AMAZING
JOURNEY

Amazing Journey

First Edition Published in Great Britain in 2016.

ISBN: 978-0-9956180-0-8

Brett Lewis can be contacted at bslewis@talk21.com
and via twitter at @bslewis1973.

Website: www.brettlewisbooks.co.uk

Cover Designed by Charlotte Mouncey.
www.bookstyle.co.uk

AMAZING JOURNEY

JOURNEY

From Ryman League Division One
North to the National League

Watching Boreham Wood FC
2008-2015

BRETT LEWIS

Borehamwood

Brett Lewis is a Recruitment Consultant, lifelong Tottenham Hotspur supporter and lover of good music. He is married to Paula and has two children, Sara and Harry.

Brett and his family moved to Borehamwood in January 2008. While at a loose end one Saturday afternoon in April 2008, he took his two year old daughter Sara to watch his local football team Boreham Wood FC for the first time. At the time, they were struggling at the wrong end of the Ryman Premier League (the seventh tier of English football) and heading for relegation to the Ryman League Division One North. What followed over the next seven years was an amazing journey in which Boreham Wood FC went on to achieve promotion to the National League (the highest division outside the Football League) for the first time in its sixty eight year history.

Amazing Journey is a personal story told by Brett Lewis about his experiences following his local football club Boreham Wood Football Club from 2008-2015 during the most successful period of its sixty seven year history.

In memory of former Boreham Wood centre back
Ryan Moran, a hell of a player and a decent bloke
who was taken from us far too early.

Also in memory of loyal Boreham Wood supporters,
Colin Lawler, Harry Ward and Geoff Wickens.
Boreham Wood Football Club is a much
poorer place without them.

Mario Noto and Greg Morgan with the
2010 Ryman Premier League Play Off winning trophy

Borehamwood players with the
2015 Conference South Promotion Final winning trophy

FOREWORD

I was delighted to be asked to write this foreword to Brett's book "Amazing Journey". The journey is indeed one I have an affinity with having followed the same journey, only from a different starting point! Let me explain.......

I was born in Boreham Wood and lived there until I was seventeen when my family moved to Kent. About seven or eight years before then, in the late 1950's, my father made the fatal mistake of taking me to watch Boreham Wood FC at our then ground in Eldon Avenue. Rather like Brett after his first visit to the club in April 2008, I was hooked. Despite marriage and a family intervening I have continued to watch the club ever since and have been an Official of the club for just over fifty years in numerous different roles.

So when Brett started his "Amazing Journey" in April 2008 I had been around a long while but had no notion of what was going to happen in the following seven years covered by this fascinating book. When I first read it so many memories came flooding back of games that had taken place and been filed away in the memory bank – after all, there were over three hundred games during those years.

However, the key events (mainly, of course, wins in two Play Off Finals) are definitely stored in the "never to be forgotten" part of the brain and they are described eloquently by Brett.

On the back cover of the book you will see a photograph of one of the flags carried around by Brett and his friends in the "Wood Army" and no foreword to the book would be complete without referring to them. It is true to say that their presence at games has made a massive difference to the Club and its players. You will read excellent descriptions by Brett of scenes of jubilation behind the goal at various games when players celebrated wildly with the "Wood Army" after a vital goal was scored.

I am sure the book will be of interest to football fans beyond those who support Boreham Wood FC, particularly anyone with a non-league involvement. It is not a straightforward narrative of 8 seasons of football watching but a very amusing story of tears, laughter, pain and then indescribable joy on Saturday 9 May 2015. The involvement of Brett's family and the references to many domestic matters adds a real human touch to the story.

Music, which is Brett's other passion, also has a unique and intriguing place in the book with fifty-one song titles being used as the chapter titles.

If I may borrow a quote from the late, great Bill Shankly, *"Some people believe that football is a matter of life or death. I am very disappointed with that attitude. I can assure you it is much, much more important than that".*

Those of us on Brett's "Amazing Journey" will agree with that, although we all know it was said tongue-in-cheek and family really are more important than football – I thought I had better add that to keep Mrs Lewis onside!

I know Brett would like me to add a few words on the growth of the club over the years and the challenges that led to the climax of the "Amazing Journey" and the impossible dream of playing in the top tier of non-league football coming true. Those challenges are initially described in our President Bill O'Neill's book on the club's history from its formation in 1948. The very existence of the club is largely down to Bill's efforts. In 1999 Danny Hunter took over the club and rebuilt the entire structure, including the creation of the much admired PASE Academy scheme. Having shared some of the many challenges with Danny, I know from first-hand experience that without his business acumen you would not be reading this book as the "Amazing Journey" would simply not have taken place.

My final word is this – having reached the holy grail of the National League it has been great to see Brett and the "Wood Army", along with their flags, in far flung parts of the country such as Barrow, Gateshead, Torquay, Tranmere and even abroad (in Wrexham, Wales!). What happened from 2015 onwards though is another story.............

Enjoy the book, I know you will!

PETER SMITH
BOREHAM WOOD FC

ACKNOWLEDGEMENT

Firstly I'd like to thank my mum because without her I probably wouldn't be here.

I would like to thank my long suffering wife Paula for allowing me to attend so many matches either with or without the kids and for her patience in me writing this book.

I would like to thank my children Sara and Harry who mean the world to me and have accompanied me to all sorts of exotic non-league grounds over the years, Harry is now my constant sidekick for home and away matches. As Sara has got older she is more interested in shopping with her mother and listening to current pop music than she is attending football matches with her old man. She still shows an interest by asking me the score after each match though.

I would like to thank Boreham Wood Chairman, Danny Hunter and Media and Communications Manager, Grant Morris for their backing and support while writing this book.

I would like to thank Danny Hunter, the management team and players at Boreham Wood Football Club for providing such fantastic entertainment and value for money over the years. It would have been impossible to write this book without the memories that they have created.

I would like to thank Boreham Wood FC club official Peter Smith for writing the Foreword and for taking the time to proof read the book. The only disadvantage of Peter's excellent proof reading is that it has made me realise how bad my English is!!

I would like to thank Boreham Wood FC Official Photographer, Sean Hinks for taking such excellent photographs during that memorable 2014-2015 season, some of which have improved this book. As memories of that season fade, these photos will act as a constant reminder of how good it was.

I would like to thank the Boreham Wood supporters, "the Wood Army" for the many friendships I've formed over the years. I can't imagine enjoying the successes of the last few years with a better group of people.

I would like to thank my good friend Paul Parry from "Paul Parry Media Services" (www.paulparry.com) for all his help, support and general advice on how to produce a book. I literally couldn't have done it without him!!

I would like to thank the legendary Pete Townshend (guitarist and songwriter from The Who) because if he hadn't written the song "Amazing Journey" for the "Tommy" album, I would have had to think of another title for this book!!

The Gaffer

CONTENTS

With Harry

With the Conference South Promotion Final winning trophy in 2015

PERFECT DAY

The events of Saturday 9th May 2015 will stay with me for the rest of my life and it was definitely the best day I've ever had as a football supporter. This was the day that "little" Boreham Wood FC made it to the National League, the fifth tier of English Football for the first time in their sixty seven year history. This was achieved with a tense but well deserved 2-1 victory over Whitehawk after extra time in the Conference South Promotion Final. The success of the team, the togetherness of players and supporters, the wild celebrations afterwards and the look of joy on my son Harry's face will take a lot of beating.

The build up to the final was tense. Having secured our place in the final with a memorable 4-2 aggregate win over Havant & Waterlooville the previous Saturday, the subsequent one week wait was a long one. In that week, the nation surprisingly voted in its first majority Conservative government since 1992 when another Coalition Government was widely predicted. Much to my amusement George Galloway and Ed Balls lost their parliamentary seats. I spent the whole week suffering from "man flu" and had had a cough for the last four weeks that I couldn't shift. As well as this, the nerve and excitement leading up to the final ensured I didn't sleep well. Harry nearly missed the greatest day of his footballing life because he initially refused to do his homework on the Friday evening. A cunning threat from my wife Paula to say "you won't be going to the match tomorrow", ensured the homework was completed with the minimum of fuss and unbelievable accuracy!!

The "perfect day" didn't start perfectly. In the morning I woke up early. In fact I hardly slept at all. Normally I'd have gone to the gym but the disease known as "man flu" stopped me. This bloody cough kept me up and I was incredibly nervous about the match, more nervous than I normally am in such situations. In the build up to the 2010 Ryman League Play off Final against Kingstonian I was excited but not this nervous. Perhaps after five more years supporting the club I was now more emotionally involved. In 2010 we scraped into the play offs so anything else was a bonus. In 2015 we should have won the league and in my opinion were a better team than Bromley who did win it. Lots of thoughts went through my head about games we should have won (or not lost). There was nothing I could do about it now. Today was the day. We had to win. Losing wasn't an option. I remember updating my Facebook profile in the morning with words such as "whatever happens, it has been a memorable season". What a load of cobblers. It would have been a massive disaster had we lost!! The team we were playing was Whitehawk. They are a science fiction character sounding football team from Brighton who were playing Sussex County League football 5 years ago. They played great football, had loads of money but had even fewer supporters than Boreham Wood did.

Having looked on the "Wood Army" Facebook group in the morning, Wood supporter Craig Payne revealed the identity of his new flag, purchased in preparation for the final. I believe it was the fourth one he'd bought in recent weeks and led me to believe he wanted to decorate the whole of Meadow Park with these bloody things!! All joking aside the slogan on the flag *Small Town, Big Dreams* was really uplifting and to be fair to Craig, it was all his idea. This summed up how close this small football club in Hertfordshire was to achieving its dreams.

I had no intention of taking the car to Meadow Park because if we won, I'd want to celebrate and if we lost I'd have needed a drink. Harry and I met a few of the boys in the Hart & Spool Pub in Borehamwood before the game. I needed a drink to calm the nerves and wanted to immerse myself in pre match banter. The place seemed to be full of Whitehawk supporters all in a jolly mood, as if the result from today didn't matter and they were there for the ride. I drank three pints fairly quickly and we all walked to the ground.

It was clear on entering the ground that this was no ordinary match. For a start there was the little matter of trying to prevent the two hundred black and white balloons from blowing away. Poor Sean Browne had to leave his half-finished pint in the bar to look after these balloons while we casually finished our drinks. The only thing that was normal about entering the ground that day was that Harry demanded some chips as soon as we got in!! We took our now usual place behind the goal. For many years Baz, Linda and I sat in the corner by the players tunnel but for the last few months of the season we decided to stand behind the goal to try and help improve the atmosphere. Also with me being incredibly superstitious, I noted that we hadn't lost a match all season when Harry and I stood behind the goal.

At 2:20 pm there were already more supporters in the ground than for a normal home league match. It was obvious this was going to eclipse the crowd we had for the play off final of 2010 which was just over 1,100 supporters, even though Kingstonian had more supporters then Whitehawk did. I remember thinking how impressive that was and how the club appeared to finally mean something to local people. The eventual crowd of 2,202 was fantastic especially as there were only about four hundred Whitehawk supporters. It amused me that when we played Whitehawk away in the 2013-2014 season the official crowd was 56! Out of the 1,800 Boreham Wood supporters here today, I'd estimate that only eight of us were at Whitehawk that day. As the players came onto the pitch we let go of the balloons and watched them either fly into the air or go on the pitch. There were plenty of pictures being taken of the home end at that time but unfortunately my face was masked by a massive bin liner as I let the balloons go. Some may argue that's a good thing!! Then a few flares were let go, some went on the pitch and one whistled past Baz's head. Thank God there weren't any smoke alarms inside the ground.

To be honest, most of the match was a blur. I was struggling with the occasion especially as the booze was wearing off and the nerves came back. I didn't enjoy the match at all despite the occasion. These were two teams who knew how to play football but there appeared to be very little of it in the first half. The only memorable moment was when a fantastic Lee Angol free kick sailed just over the bar as I was getting Harry a hot dog (he was still hungry after the chips). As the second half started I remember thinking, one goal would win this. Whoever scored first could easily shut up shop and see this out. Despite Whitehawk's pretty passing (Kissock and Deering looked good) they didn't look like offering much up front.

In the sixty seventh minute we had a free kick in "Lee Angol territory". He just missed one in the first half but scored excellent free kicks in recent weeks against Sutton United and Chelmsford. Surely this was his moment. The other free kicks had sailed into the top corner and Whitehawk keeper Craig Ross was lining up his wall for this eventuality. Suddenly Lee Angol appears to role the ball along the ground towards the other corner. 1-0 to Boreham Wood!! The ground went berserk and Lee Angol ran towards the supporters behind the goal which has been a constant theme of the season (players and supporters celebrating together). This was Lee Angol's thirty second and most important goal of a great season. The sixty seventh minute was exactly the same time that the late Ryan Moran (God bless him) scored the opening goal in the 2010 play-off final against Kingstonian. There was no way back for them that day. Surely there was no way back for "The Hawks" now. Our defence had seen out games like this all season and indeed we'd often added a second goal to make sure. Hold on, there are twenty three minutes left plus stoppage time, which always seems to be loads when you don't want it to be. You can add five minutes of injury time to that! Every minute will seem like an hour. My bold prediction that one goal would win it was still on my mind. "We'll definitely see this out". The Gaffer replaced Graeme Montgomery with Matty Whichelow. Good call as he can use his pace and hold the ball up in the corner.

Despite the anxiety, the clock seemed to go down quite quickly. There were seven minutes left on the clock when the dangerous Whitehawk midfielder Kissock was in our penalty box though appearing to be going nowhere and took a tumble (or was fouled) under challenge from midfielder Sam Cox, the referee points to the spot. Having seen Cox in over a hundred games for Boreham Wood, I know he never makes a tackle unless it's absolutely necessary or unless he is 100% sure of winning it. There is no way he would have made such a tackle in the box at such a critical time in such an important game. Would he? Sam Deering made no mistake from the spot and it was 1-1. There was no doubt that we were shell shocked at this point. Whitehawk were suddenly on the ascendancy and looking the most likely team to win it. As I previously predicted, there were five minutes of injury time. In the first of those minutes, we had a massive let off. Former Boreham Wood defender Osei Sankofa somehow shot over from six yards out when it was easier to score. That would have won it. There is no way we were coming back from that. We were gone and needed the whistle to blow so the players could regroup for extra time. It you had offered me penalties at that point I would have snapped your hand off. To my mind, Sankofa's miss was the only bit of luck we'd had all season. When you think of all the things that didn't go our way (more about that later) I believe that this miss made up for all of them. Perhaps it really does even out over the season.

The whistle blew for the end of full time. The players sat down and got a pep talk from the Manager, followed by a group hug. That hug actually lifted me. I suddenly felt that although we were "gone" in the last few minutes of normal time, that hug meant something to a group of players who had been through so much together and just needed one final push to make all our dreams come true. At this point Harry needed the toilet and being "Mr Independent" insisted on going alone. In light of what was about to happen, thank God he did!! Extra time then started and I wasn't really paying attention. My cough was pretty bad at that point and I had just made my fortieth trip to the bin to dispose of yet another used tissue. What happened next was a bit of a blur but before I knew it, we were 2-1 up. It was down the other end and I hadn't realized who scored. I thought it was Ricky Shakes at first. All I remember was Ben Nunn crossing it in from the right to Lee Angol. The scorer was actually Junior Morias who buried Angol's nod down into the corner past Craig Ross. The celebrations were a bit more low key this time as people were still taking up their positions for extra time and it was at the other end so the celebrating with supporters that had been such a feature of the season hadn't happened on this occasion. The partnership between former Wycombe duo Angol and Morias which had worked so well for over a year, struck again at the most crucial time. Harry having missed the goal, returned from the toilet a few minutes later. When I told him what had happened, he punched the air in delight and gave me a cuddle.

During normal time we had twenty three minutes to hold out. Now we had twenty nine minutes. "I'm not sure how much of this I can take". I felt like spending the next twenty nine minutes sat on the toilet with my hands over my ears!! Surely we weren't going to let this slip again. The only thing I really remembered about the rest of extra time was Junior Morias and Sam Cox getting injured and a seemingly lengthy stop in play so they could get treatment. I remembered Ricky Shakes chasing every ball and not giving their full-back any peace, like he'd done all season. The clock seemed to tick down nice and quickly and the inevitable Whitehawk counter attack didn't happen. Unfortunately the third Boreham Wood goal didn't occur either but as the clock ticked down we were winning every header, clearing every ball and the tippy tappy Whitehawk football didn't look like getting them a goal. During this period, Wood supporter Iain Barnfield sang the same bloody song over and over again for about twenty minutes. I didn't know whether to clobber him or join in. I decided to join in when I saw fit, purely to while away the time. In the end, I left Iain to it although I'm surprised he had a voice left by the end of it. I certainly didn't. We were nearly home and dry. The Boreham Wood supporters around us were positioning themselves for the inevitable dash onto the pitch which usually occurs at this level of football in such circumstances.

The boy Harry had been excited about going on the pitch ever since he saw the Aston Villa supporters do it recently on television when they beat West Bromwich Albion in the FA Cup. I told him that we'd gone on the pitch when we won the play offs in 2010 and he was fascinated by it. In fact he was disappointed we didn't go on the "hallowed turf" when we won the semi-final against Havant & Waterlooville the week before. I was beginning to think that going on the pitch was more important to him then actually winning the match and getting promoted. With extra time nearly up, everyone was getting ready. Harry now couldn't see a thing as all these much taller people were standing in front of him. Then referee Anthony Coggins put the whistle to his mouth and blew up. WE DID IT. I remember hugging Harry, Linda and Baz. We'd seen so many games together over the years. I also hugged Phil Jackson who had hardly missed a game at Boreham Wood since 1980 and could remember every single one. I lifted Harry over the fence and climbed over myself to get on the pitch. The Boreham Wood supporters seemed to get on the pitch easily. It's not surprising when one hundred and eighty-three of us had to scale the fence at St Albans in January. More about that later!

The scenes at the final whistle were incredible, grown men and women hugging each other, jumping up and down and screaming with joy. I shook the gaffer, Ian Allinson's hand and hugged Luke Garrard and Mario Noto (Assistant Manager and First Team Coach). I then spotted right-back Ben Nunn and was about to descend on him when his tearful mother got there first. I did the right thing and left them to it. For the next few minutes it was a case of getting as many hugs and high fives in as I could with players and supporters while watching Harry, really excited about winning and being on the pitch. Having acknowledged a few people I knew in the stand, we were then advised to clear the pitch while the trophy ceremony was being prepared. Harry and I climbed back over the fence into the stand. I was keen to get over to the East stand for the medal ceremony as soon as possible and asked Harry to "hurry up" and get over the fence. This led to three of our fellow supporters singing the words to "Hurry up Harry" in singing voices that would have disgusted legendary "Sham 69" front man *Jimmy Pursey had he been there. Once we were over the fence, Harry and I* made our way round to the East Stand in preparation for the ceremony while a number of supporters left the ground and presumably went home. I couldn't understand this. Had this been supporters of clubs in the FA Cup Final no one would have left. Perhaps being a part time supporter of their local club didn't have the same appeal.

Having walked round to the East Stand, it was nice to congratulate Bill O'Neill, founder of the club and former Chairman who was eighty seven years old and still in very good health. I bet when he was building this ground brick by brick in the early 1960's he didn't think that promotion to the fifth tier of English football was possible. The trophy and medal ceremony was fairly long but interesting. Every player and the backroom staff was called individually to collect their medals and stand behind a branded "Vanarama Conference South Promotion Final Winners" placard. When the last player, Captain Callum Reynolds went to collect the trophy, the whole place erupted. What a fantastic moment and a wonderful experience for those who were there. It was nice to see Greg Morgan get a medal after 350+ games for Boreham Wood even though he'd been on loan elsewhere for most of the season. This home grown player had contributed so much to the club over the years and when I started watching them in 2008 he was the first player who really stood out for me. Although nothing had been confirmed, I assumed he'd played his last match for the club. After about twenty minutes of pictures with the trophy the players returned to the dressing room and we headed for the bar.

At this point I felt absolutely drained. Walking into a very jubilant but very warm bar the heat hit me. As well as being quite a warm day, it was extremely busy. There seemed no way of getting to the bar and to be honest I didn't really want an alcoholic drink at this point. I was much more interested in sitting outside and demolishing the two bottles of water I had in my bag. Harry and I sat on the bench for a while talking to people, savouring what had just been achieved while trying to feel more energetic. By 7pm Harry wanted to go home. The occasion had got to him and he was feeling tired and getting quite moody. It's easy to forget he was still only six years old. This was Harry's thirty third match of the season and I'm sure this match and the season will live long in the memory for him as it will for the rest of us. I can't imagine many of his mates have experienced what he witnessed that day. I called Paula to pick him up but while we waited, we went in the bar. It was slightly more bearable. Harry was collected soon afterwards and I remained in the bar to enjoy the evening's celebrations.

Quite soon afterwards the players came into the bar with the trophy with the sound of "Tom Hark" by "The Piranhas" blaring out loudly. At this point there was plenty of singing, plenty of photos being taken with the players and the trophy, lots of good banter and plenty of booze being drunk. It was a good opportunity to speak to some of the players about our achievements. I started to feel less drained and was ready to keep going. The rest of the evening seems to go quickly. I remember seeing the Chairman, Danny Hunter for the first time since the match and having a long conversation with him as well as what seemed like my thousandth man hug of the day. None of this would have been possible without him. At about 9pm I went to McDonalds to feed my face before returning in double quick time. When I left the bar at 12:30am there were still a few people there but I was feeling ill, rough and drunk. We'd cleaned the bar out of draught lager. As I was leaving, I seem to remember the Chairman asking me if I wanted to take the trophy home. I declined as I didn't want to risk leaving it in a cab. Can you imagine the uproar that would have caused? On reflection, I should have taken it. I'd have spent the next hour taking "selfies" with the trophy. I'm sure Paula wouldn't have minded sharing our marital bed with it!!

Following this wonderful achievement, the Boreham Wood squad went on a well earnt break to Puerto Banus and some of the supporters continued the celebrations a couple of weeks later at Gill and Terry Cox's house (Sam Cox parents) who very kindly hosted an afternoon/evening for us. I took the trophy with me as it was a great opportunity for supporters who weren't in the bar after the match to have photos taken with it. This was an excellent way to continue the celebrations with plenty of decent food, beer and a load of classic ska and reggae music.

A few weeks later I was watching Barcelona play Atletico Madrid live on Sky and the commentary team including Northern Ireland legend Gerry Armstrong were talking about examples of close play off finishes when Armstrong said "like Whitehawk losing in extra time". I was gobsmacked. Where did that come from?

To sum up a day like this, I remembered a quote from the end of Rocky II when he has won the World Heavyweight Title by beating Apollo Creed. Rocky said during the interview afterwards *"except for my kid being born, this is the greatest night in the history of my life"*

Days like the 9th May 2015 didn't just happen. There is a long story behind it going back a number of years.

We did it!!

INTRODUCTION

Start

I've never written a book before but as I've heard many times "everyone's got a book in them". I never thought that saying would apply to me until now. I've always thought that if I wrote a book, it would be about either one of my two favourite interests, football or music. It would also have to be non-fiction as I don't have a particularly good imagination.

I have decided to write about football and my first seven years of watching my local football team, Boreham Wood FC, and explain how a massive Spurs supporter with no previous interest in non-league football, can suddenly develop a real passion for his local football club in what just happened to be the most successful period in its sixty seven year history. In that time, the club went from relegation to the Ryman League Division One North, to promotion to the National League (formerly the Conference National), the fifth tier of English Football three divisions above. To add a music theme to the book, I have decided to name each chapter after a descriptive song which would form a particularly impressive soundtrack if this book becomes a film!!

The title of this book says it all. The period from 2008 to 2015 has been an "amazing journey" for Boreham Wood Football Club and for me personally. The subtitle is a bit misleading though as we never actually played in the "Ryman League Division One North" during this period despite being relegated to that division. Why? It's a long story, to go with a number of other long stories in this book.

Why?

Perhaps it's a "midlife crisis". Some people in that situation get tattoos, some buy flash cars they can't afford and some run off with women twenty years their junior! I, on the other hand have decided to write a book!! (I can't find a woman twenty years my junior who would have me!!). Apart from "The History of Boreham Wood Football Club" by the club founder and current Club President Bill O'Neill which came out in 2005, no other book about the football club has ever been written as far as I know. Although Bill O'Neill's book isn't readily available, I recently read it, having been lent a copy by Boreham Wood Chairman, Danny Hunter. Although it's a fascinating read, it was released over ten years ago and therefore doesn't cover the period since 2005, the most successful in Boreham Wood's history. In a lot of ways, "Amazing Journey" picks up where Bill O'Neill's book left off. By the way, it's always great to see Bill around the club, attending matches and speaking at our End of Season Presentation Nights and looking so well despite being in his late eighties.

There is also a book called "Far From the Massive Crowd" by Mark Cowan that follows the fortunes of Guisborough Town in the Northern League Division Two in the 2010-2011 season. It's ironic that this title could have been given to this book due to Boreham Wood FC's legendary low crowds. Having read the book, it did get me thinking "wouldn't it be nice if there was a similar book about Boreham Wood FC", not just about one season but about several seasons. I think that the story of a small football club in a small town, making it to the fifth tier of English football is definitely worth writing about. The book will hopefully give people a flavour of not only the progress made on the pitch but off it too. There is no doubt, that Boreham Wood FC in 2015 was a very different football club to the one I start watching in 2008.

At the end of 2014, I started an unofficial Facebook group for supporters and as members of this group started sharing their memories, I thought about my memories of watching the club and started writing things down. For no apparent reason, I started to write about our day in Brighton just before Christmas in 2013 when we played Whitehawk although I didn't know what I was going to do with it at the time. Sometime later I started to add other things and the next thing I knew I had the makings of a book. The story had to have a happy ending and fortunately it did with promotion to the National League in 2015. I'm conscious that this thought process was some time ago and my initial plan to complete the book by the summer of 2015 was a little ambitious to say the least. I failed to appreciate how difficult the process would be and how much time I had to commit to writing. I also underestimated the work required once I'd finished writing, for example, the editing, proof reading, setting up the website, formatting and designing the cover. Having a young family and a busy full time job meant that I only had limited time to spend on all of this. I initially planned to add the 2015-16 season to it but it would have been a bit too longwinded and probably sent half of you to sleep. There is no reason that can't be the subject of another book in the not too distant future.

If you work for the club and are reading this book, don't worry, there isn't anything controversial in it and any sensitive private conversations I may have had with people over the years will remain private. I certainly don't plan to alienate anyone at the club and hope they will enjoy the book like everyone else. In any case, it's hard to find too much fault with people who run a football club that had been on the up since 2008. Boreham Wood FC is run fantastically well by people who have created a formula that should act as a blueprint for other clubs of similar size with a limited fan base. If at times I am critical of certain people in this book, it's nothing personal. I have just written it as I see it. In any case, anyone I've criticised is almost certainly no longer associated with the club anyway. I just want to give a flavour of what it's like to watch the team home and away as a supporter, while giving a light hearted and tongue in cheek account of my experiences while giving a chronological account of each season as well as my opinion on matches, players, great goals, poor crowds and different events that have shaped this period at Boreham Wood Football Club.

Hopefully this book will appeal not just to Boreham Wood or non-league fans but to football fans in general. It might even appeal to those with no interest in "the beautiful game".

Strange Town

Borehamwood is a town in South Hertfordshire on the outskirts of Greater London. In the 2011 census it had a population of 37,065. Elstree and Borehamwood railway station is located on the Thameslink route from Bedford to Brighton via London and offers a frequent service to Central London and the City as well as Luton and Gatwick Airports.

Following World War II, the town's population greatly increased, with large areas of council housing built for displaced Londoners, many of which are now in private ownership. The fast train connections to Central London has resulted in the town becoming a residential suburb. Borehamwood is currently undergoing another substantial housing transformation which has seen hundreds of new homes built over the last few years and many more on their way. Borehamwood is probably best known for its film and TV studios, known as Elstree Studios, often referred to as "The British Hollywood". It has seen a number of classic films including, The Dam Busters, Summer Holiday, Dr Zhivago and 2001 A Space Odyssey as well as the first three Indiana Jones films and the first three Star Wars movies. As for TV programmes, it is currently the home of *Eastenders, Holby City, Big Brother* and *Strictly Come Dancing*. Previously it produced *Auf Wiedersehn Pet, Grange Hill* and *Who Wants to be a Millionaire*.

Empire Building

Boreham Wood Football Club was formed in 1948 following the amalgamation of Boreham Rovers and Royal Retournez. They played on Meadow Road for one season before moving to Eldon Avenue which was the clubs home until it returned to Meadow Park (and its current home) in 1963.

In 1966, after playing in leagues such as the Mid-Herts League, Spartan League and Parthenon League, they joined the Athenian League, where two promotions took them to the top division, where they were champions in 1973–74. After this, the team joined the Isthmian League (Ryman league). In 1977 they reached the Isthmian League Premier Division having secured the Division One Championship. The club then had a five season spell in the Premier Division during the late seventies and early eighties, and enjoyed an-other much more successful spell in the Premier Division in the nineties.

Over the years the club has had many successes in cup competitions including two journeys to the FA Cup Second Round in 1996-97 and 1997–98 and a memorable run to the semi – final of the FA Trophy in 2005-06. Before 2008 they had won the Herts Senior Cup four times as well as the London FA Senior Challenge Cup and Isthmian League Cup.

Before 1999 the club Chairman was Phil Wallace, the CEO of Lamex Foods (formerly L+M Foods). He had taken over the club after the long Bill O'Neill era ended in 1991. During the 1990's the club had some notable cup runs and a brief flirtation with promotion from the Isthmian Premier division to the Football Conference (now The National League) in 1998 finishing second to Kingstonian, missing out on promotion as only one team went up in those days. In the summer of 1999 Phil Wallace sold the club to local businessman Danny Hunter. Wallace went on to have amazing success as the Chairman of Stevenage Borough. Danny Hunter was a successful Prop Master in the film industry and no stranger to Boreham Wood Football Club as his late father Micky Hunter was Manager during a successful period in the late Sixties and early Seventies. Danny Hunter therefore spent a lot of his childhood at Meadow Park. It was very clear to the new Chairman that the football club could no longer survive at Ryman League level on meagre crowds and dwindling hospitality income so he had to introduce other revenue streams to the club to boost its income and run it like a business.

In 2001 Danny Hunter introduced the P.A.S.E. Scheme (Programme for Academic and Sporting Excellence) that has no doubt provided a sound base for the club's future. The PASE programme included a link up with Oakland College to create a Football Education Scheme for 16–19 year olds. This started with only sixteen boys and has since become the largest and most successful scheme of its kind in the United Kingdom. There are now over five hundred scholars based in two locations with a successful link up with Barnet & Southgate College. The scheme has produced a number of Football

League and semi-professional footballers. Over the years it has also provided full time coaching opportunities for a number of the first team squad. Clearly someone coaching the next generation of kids during the week, will have more of an affinity with the club and this should have the desired effect with their performance on a Saturday. During the same period the club's stadium facilities were upgraded considerably and there was a state of the art artificial pitch built which also brought much needed income into the club.

All wasn't well on the pitch in Danny Hunter's first season and the team was relegated to Ryman League Division One finishing second from bottom of the table in the 1999-2000 season. However, the club was immediately promoted to the Premier Division as Division One Champions in the 2000/2001 season under Graham Roberts. In 2004 the FA engineered a restructuring of Non-League Football with the introduction of the Conference North and Conference South (now National League's North and South) and as part of these changes further down the football pyramid, Boreham Wood FC was moved to the Southern League Division One East. Under Manager Steve Cook and Director of Football Ian Allinson, the 2005-2006 season was the most successful season in the clubs history to date. Not only did they win the Southern League Division One East Title but had an amazing cup run, all the way to the Semi Final of the FA Trophy, the lowest ranked team ever to go that far. As a result of that promotion and further restructuring, the club returned to play in the Ryman Football League Premier Division in the 2006/07 season finishing a creditable seventh place just outside the playoffs. Unfortunately the 2007-08 season didn't build on the success of recent years and despite doing the double over AFC Wimbledon, Steve Cook was sacked and by the time I watched my first game against Carshalton Athletic on 19th

April 2008, the club was flirting with relegation and seventh from bottom of a league with four clubs due to be relegated.

Young and Innocent Days

The FA Cup win of 1981 did it for me. As soon as Ricky Villa scored that fantastic winner against Manchester City, it was Tottenham Hotspur all the way for me. Like many Spurs supporters at the time, my favourite player was Glenn Hoddle. I became a very enthusiastic armchair supporter watching Spurs win the FA Cup again in 1982 followed by the UEFA Cup in 1984 after a dramatic penalty shootout in the Final against Anderlecht at White Hart Lane. In 1985 Spurs were genuine challengers for the League Championship before losing out to Howard Kendall's Everton. This is the first time in my life that Tottenham have challenged for the league title!! I can't believe I had to wait another thirty years for a team I support to challenge for a title and this time it wouldn't be Tottenham.

My first live match was the North London Derby just after Christmas 1982 at Highbury. Unfortunately, I was taken by my Arsenal supporting uncle and made to stand in the North Bank. Spurs lost 2-0 with Alan Sunderland and Tony Woodcock scoring for Arsenal. As I had no one to take me to football on a regular basis, I spent the next couple of years of my football education watching "Match of the Day" and "The Big Match" on TV as well as the occasional live league game that started appearing on television around this time. My first experience of regular live football was getting the train with my brother Elliot to watch a rather entertaining Watford team in the mid 1980's. I stood on the Family Terrace with all the other spotty kids watching the likes of John Barnes and Luther Blissett play and scoring goals for fun. My other brother Alex who had no interest in football, ironically now goes to watch Watford home and away.

It was a number of years until I actually watched Spurs again. My first trip to White Hart Lane was during our "nearly season" of 1986-87 (3rd in the league, FA Cup finalist and League Cup Semi Finalist) when I went with a friend and his dad on a Wednesday night to watch Spurs beat Leicester City 5-0 at White Hart Lane. This match was four days before the Second Leg of the League Cup Semi Final against Arsenal. In the first leg at Highbury, a Clive Allen goal gave Tottenham a deserved 1-0 victory. When Clive Allen scored again in the first half of the 2nd leg giving Spurs a 2-0 aggregate lead what could possible go wrong? During half time, the PA announcer gave details of purchasing Cup Final tickets for Spurs fans!! Inevitably two second half goals from Arsenal took the game to a replay (no penalty shoot outs then). Having won the toss for home advantage in the replay, another Clive Allen goal gave Spurs the lead which they held until the eighty third minute. Then a nippy winger called Ian Allinson came off the bench to score the equaliser and supply the winner for the late David Rocastle in stoppage time to send Arsenal to Wembley. I was a heartbroken thirteen year old that night and not only was it one of my worst experiences as a Spurs fan, I also see that as a turning point in the history of the two North London clubs consigning Spurs to nearly thirty years of second best. A couple of months later I had an even worse day. I got a ticket for the FA Cup Final where hot favourites Tottenham lost to Coventry City.

As a fourteen year old in 1988, I was now old enough to go to football on my own or with friends. I took up Junior Spurs membership and attended most home games and occasional away matches. At that time Spurs signed Paul Gascoigne and the football we played over the next three years was incredible, culminating in our FA Cup win in 1991 soon after beating Arsenal in the semi-final at Wembley (my best day in football before May 2015). Had I known that for the next twenty five years (and counting), Spurs would never appear in the FA Cup Final again, losing six Semi-Finals in the process, I would have probably been sick!

From 1993 to 1996, I was at University in Birmingham so I rarely watched Spurs at home but attended many away games in the Midlands and North. At the time, Gold and Sullivan (and Barry Fry) livened up Birmingham City and Big Ron was winning things at Aston Villa. West Bromwich Albion and Wolverhampton Wanderers were mid table second tier teams so I tended to go there once a year when Watford played them (with my brother Alex). With Walsall and Coventry thrown into the mix, there was plenty of live football to watch.

When I graduated in 1996 and got my first full time job, I spent the following two years only making occasional trips to White Hart Lane as I worked most Saturdays. However in 1998, I got my first ever season ticket which I held until 2004. Those six years were fairly uneventful. They did include a League Cup Final win against Leicester in 1999 and a League Cup Final defeat against Blackburn in 2002 but not a lot else. By 2004 my priorities had changed. I was now a married man and we were about to start a family. My money would be better spent elsewhere than in Daniel Levy's deep pocket. Since 2004 I have only been an occasional visitor to White Hart Lane and while still a passionate supporter, I'd rather watch the games from my armchair. In the last year or so, my son Harry has been keen to watch Spurs when Boreham Wood haven't played so we have gone a few times but in truth I don't miss going regularly. The expense, the traffic getting there and back, the walk to and from where we park and the time it takes to get out of the ground were things I was happy to see the back of. From 2005 when my daughter Sara was born it would have been harder to be out of the house for so long on a Saturday or Sunday. I was convinced that when I gave up my season ticket in 2004 that I would be back. Perhaps I would get a season ticket with my kids when they are old enough. This is now very unlikely.

Before 2008 non-league football to me meant sub-standard football played by pub players in front of crap crowds and lots of hoofing the ball up the field. It was against everything I believed in. I'd growth up the "Spurs Way". I was daft enough to think this before 2008. In reality the "Spurs way" actually meant playing second fiddle to Arsenal, losing six semi Finals in a row and never actually winning anything of note. Non-league football was something I could never appreciate. Despite that, I had a passing interest at odd times in my life. My local club Wealdstone won The Alliance League (now the National League) and FA Trophy double in 1985. They were the first club ever to do this. Unfortunately this was just before automatic promotion to the Football League began. What a difference it would have made to Wealdstone to play in the Football League.

I was intrigued about another local team, Barnet under Barry Fry, always seemed to come second in the Conference when automatic promotion to the Football League was established in 1986. However they finally achieved promotion in 1991 by winning the Conference League Title. I was fortunate enough to watch Barnet in their last home game of that season against Welling United at Underhill. Barnet needed to win to give themselves a chance of promotion, and a Gary Bull penalty with five minutes to go sealed a well-deserved 3-2 win in a pulsating match. A mass pitch invasion occurred at the final whistle in which a burly six feet four inch seventeen year old at his first non-league game attempted to jump on Barry Fry's back in celebration. Perhaps this non-league football lark wasn't so bad after all.

I was too engrossed in Tottenham Hotspur to note the rapid decline of Wealdstone Football Club and Barnet's first stay in league football which ended in 2001 with relegation back to the Conference. I attended the FA Trophy Final in 1998 with a mate who supported Southport. Unfortunately they lost after extra time in a dreadful match against Cheltenham Town. At the end of the 2003-2004 season, I made my second ever trip to Underhill to watch Barnet in the Conference Play Off Semi Final against hot favourites Shrewsbury Town. Having watched Spurs regularly that year, I have to admit this was easily the best game of football I saw that season. Barnet won it with the last kick off the game and the noise inside Underhill that night was deafening. Seventeen year old goalkeeper, Joe Hart was on the Shrewsbury Town bench that night.

Something Got Me Started

I knew almost nothing about Boreham Wood FC before 2008. I knew they had a football team. I also knew that one of my football heroes Graham Roberts had been their manager at one time. I was aware that one of my anti-heroes Ian Allinson had held the same position. Since I've been watching Boreham Wood, I've heard a number of stories about the famous FA Trophy run in 2006 which I knew nothing about it. I knew nothing about the FA Cup runs of the 1990's. In fact when I went to my first game in April 2008, I hadn't researched any of their players and didn't even know what league the team were in. The only thing I knew was that they were in a relegation scrap.

When we moved to Borehamwood from Bushey in January 2008, it wasn't a strange place to me. (even though it is a strange place). I had uncles and grandparents living in the area and regularly used to visit them. We also had some close friends living there. I was well aware of the edgy part of "The Wood" which I rather liked. It reminded me of where I lived in Birmingham as a student (apart from the lack of decent pubs and curry houses!!). It's fair to say, I felt at home as soon as we moved there.

On the evening of Friday 18th April 2008, Paula and I were in our kitchen debating what to do over the weekend with our two year old daughter Sara, when I spotted a promotion in the Borehamwood Times. It was from Boreham Wood Football Club offering tickets for the final two home games of the season for only £2 (for both) with children going FREE. Apparently they were in relegation trouble and quite rightly wanted to get as many people as possible through the turnstile to help improve the atmosphere. The first of these games was on the Saturday against Carshalton Athletic followed by Staines Town on the Tuesday night, both at home and both included in this promotion. The final match of the season (not included in this promotion) was away at Ramsgate the following Saturday. Paula and I were both keen for me to take Sara. I wanted to watch a live game and Paula wanted the afternoon to herself. Although Paula was only three months pregnant with Harry at the time, it was obviously getting too much for her.

The following afternoon, Paula dropped us at the club and my first impressions of it weren't great. There weren't many people there despite the cheap entry and the relegation battle. The atmosphere was flat and I remember being disappointed that the town appeared to have given up on its local football team. I have always been amazed at the apathy towards Boreham Wood FC from the local people. Surely any other town would back their local club in such circumstances particularly if they only had to pay £2 to get in for two matches. This makes a mockery of comments I've heard from local people since who have said that if the club reduced prices, more people would come to games. This match in April 2008 is proof that it isn't the case. There doesn't seem to be the community spirit in Borehamwood as there is in other towns. There are just a collection of individuals doing their own thing. Perhaps it was this that attracted me to the club, a sense that I could contribute to something when no one else could be bothered. It certainly wasn't the football that attracted me as the match was shocking and ended 0-0 with Carshalton missing a penalty. Both sides were lucky to get nil. This game was played five days after the club won the Herts Senior Cup Final by beating Ware at Letchworth's County Ground. They had also won two out of their last three league games so were heading into this fixture in relatively good form. I remember pushing Sara's buggy around the ground about fourteen times and her climbing the steps next to where the players come out, sitting near a fierce looking bloke who despite that was quite friendly. I later found out his name was Mo. The Boreham Wood Manager that day was George Borg and his language was a bit colourful. Borg had an interesting history as a Non-League manager which came to an abrupt end in 2014 when as Enfield Town Manager he was alleged to have used abusive and/or indecent and/or insulting words towards Wingate and Finchley FC supporters. In 2008 he was charged with keeping Boreham Wood in the Ryman Premier League having taken over from Steve Cook three months earlier. He appeared to be struggling with this task. There was only one player on show for Boreham Wood who I recognised and that was defender Ollie Adedeji. I remember that while he was an Aldershot Town player some years before, I tried to find him a job.

Despite this negativity, I saw something that day to convince me to get a season ticket for the following season. Sara loved it as it was a bit different (and she was too young to know any better). Having been without a season ticket at football since giving up my Spurs one four years earlier, I missed going to live football. Perhaps this would fill the void. I knew I wouldn't get another Spurs season ticket for the foreseeable future with a two year old and another one on the way. In that case, why not support a local team instead? Its five minutes from home and a season ticket wouldn't cost that much for both of us.

The Carshalton match was followed by a 2-0 defeat on the Tuesday against Staines Town which I didn't attend. The club were now sailing close to the wind with the final match away at Ramsgate. Borg had already gone by then. Boreham Wood only needed to avoid defeat by more than three goals to stay up and other results had to go against them. Surely they were safe. That Saturday I paid little attention to Boreham Wood's plight but decided to check online just after 5 pm to find out the score. I was shocked to discover that a comprehensive 5-0 defeat and other results going against them, meant they were relegated. I can't even imagine the atmosphere amongst the supporters that day. Were there any supporters there? How could the players expect to get motivated with no support? I have been to many "End of Season Presentation Nights" but this is one I'm pleased I missed. Despite relegation, I was still getting a season ticket. I wasn't yet emotionally involved enough to care too much about what league we were in. I actually called the club two weeks later (while I was at Lords watching England play New Zealand in a Test Match) to enquire how much season tickets were. The chap answering the phone said that they hadn't set the prices yet and to try again in a few weeks. His tone suggested that he was actually saying "what do you want to get a season ticket for this shower of shit for?" I was preparing to start my first season as a Boreham Wood season ticket holder watching the team in the eighth tier of English Football playing the likes of Great Wakering Rovers and Maldon Town! However it didn't quite work out that way.

It was quite obvious I didn't back a winning horse in 2008. Fortunately the horse I backed subsequently became a winning horse.

2008-2009 SEASON

Knock On Wood

Having assumed I would be watching Boreham Wood FC in the Ryman League Division One North, I was pleasantly surprised to find out that they were reprieved from relegation, staying in the Ryman Premier Division instead. Despite the players best efforts, the final day heartache at Ramsgate and the 5-0 thrashing, didn't end up getting the club relegated after all. How was this possible? The answer lies with Halifax Town Football Club!!

Halifax Town from West Yorkshire was founded in 1911 and became an established Football League club from 1923 to 1993. They are famous for beating the mighty Manchester United in a pre-season tournament in 1971 and knocking Malcolm Allison's big spending Manchester City out of the FA Cup in 1980. In May 2008 Halifax, now a Conference club went bust with debts of £2million, owing £800,000 to the taxman. FA rules state that if a club reforms, they must start at least two divisions lower and the newly formed FC Halifax Town took their place in the Northern Premier League Division One for the 2008-09 season. How did events at a faraway northern football club affect the immediate future of a small Hertfordshire club two hundred miles away? The answer is surprisingly straight forward. Due to Halifax's demise, four levels of non-league football had a relegation place taken away to even up each league. Altrincham (Conference Premier), Hucknall Town (Conference North), Slough

Town (BGB Southern League Division One South & West) and Boreham Wood (Ryman Premier Division) were all reprieved from relegation. Boreham Wood happened to have the highest points total of the relegated teams at their level in the football pyramid hence the reprieve. Confused? So am I. Who cares? We were safe. How ironic that the newly formed FC Halifax Town was to be Boreham Wood's first opponents in the National League some seven years later.

Following the club's reprieve from the relegation, I bought mine and Sara's first season tickets. When it arrived, it contained a free ticket for the Boreham Wood Vs Arsenal pre-season match. A generous gesture but how dare they. There was no way I was watching that. "How can I sit amongst those people". In fact I avoided this fixture for the first three seasons and didn't go to my first pre-season game against Arsenal until 2011. I was a bit childish in 2008!! I had no idea at the time about the relationship between the clubs. Having eventually become aware, I learnt to grin and bear it

With George Borg and most of the team from the 2007–2008 season gone, a new manager was appointed. Ian Allinson, the man who broke my heart all those years ago, returned for his third spell at the club (he was previously Manager and then Director of Football). Allinson was a vastly experienced Manager at non-league level and as well as Boreham Wood, he also had spells at Barton Rovers, Stotfold and Baldock Town where he converted a young right back called Kevin Phillips to a centre forward role. The rest was history. I suppose, the Chairman wanted someone he knew well and trusted to rebuild the squad, avoiding the situation the club found themselves in the previous season. Allinson was assisted by David McDonald (former Spurs and Republic of Ireland player) as his number two. I remember watching McDonald play for Spurs at Anfield against Liverpool all those years ago. I'd hoped he was a better coach than he was a player!! Allinson overhauled the squad with the likes of Marvin Samuel, Steve Wales and Chris Bangura leaving and the main striker Simon Thomas joining Crystal Palace. In came Mario Noto from Chelmsford, Lee Allinson (Ian's son), Jon Wordsworth and Wes Daly amongst others. Mario Noto was easily the best player we had in my first three years supporting the club. The squad had a fresher feel to it and started the season in impressive form.

The season started with a 2-1 win victory at Tooting & Mitchum and a 2-0 home win against Hastings. I didn't attend either match. I had no intention in those days of going to away games. Sara and I made our debuts as season ticket holders the following Saturday at Meadow Park against Ramsgate in a hard fought 1-1 draw. The second match we attended, was an entertaining 3-2 defeat against eventual champions Dover Athletic who brought a massive crowd. I was surprised that former Watford and Gillingham player Andy Hessenthaler was marshalling the midfield for Dover as Player Manager.

In September, long serving goalkeeper Noel Imber left the club suddenly and was replaced in goal by Anthony Anstead who joined from Cheshunt. I'm still not sure what caused this sudden parting of the ways. Apart from a couple of errors that led to goals against Sutton United later in the season, I don't think Anstead let us down even though he was eventually dropped in favour of Simon Overland. The Carshalton game was far better than the one I watched in April and the 2-0 victory was well deserved. The team had a good little run in September and October winning several league matches. They also managed to win 5-0 at Conference South side Thurrock in the Second Qualifying round of the FA Cup with goals from Wordsworth, Lee Allinson, Leon Archer (2) and Chris Watters.

The 5th October, the day after a 1-1 draw at Harrow Borough marked the arrival of an individual who within three years was to attend Boreham Wood matches home and away on a regular basis. My son Harry was born. After a fairly long labour, Paula came up with the goods in the early hours of the morning and we now had a son to go with our three year old daughter Sara. The mayhem caused by the arrival of another child meant that the following Saturday's FA Cup exit at home to Brackley Town in the Third Qualifying Round of the FA Cup didn't register. I didn't go to the game and didn't find out the score until the next day. The following Tuesday night, I was allowed to attend the Ashford Town (Middlesex) home game which we won 3-1. At this stage we were seventh in the table and nine points behind leaders Dover Athletic. The change in Manager and half the squad seemed to be working. We had old heads like Ollie Adedeji and Lee Harvey and a younger Jon Wordsworth in defence, Daly, Allinson, Watters and Noto were impressive in midfield and we had the likes of Leon Archer and Elliot Buchanan upfront. The player who most impressed me was Greg Morgan. I liked the way this local PASE academy graduate was running at defenders and his ball control and his skills belonged at a higher level. Unfortunately Greg Morgan wasn't the only player to lose form towards the end of the season as the team started to slide down the table. At this stage of the season my "first love" Tottenham Hotspur were sitting bottom of the Premier League with two points from eight matches, the worst start by any club in Premier League history. Fortunately for Spurs, their fortunes were about to change, following the appointment of Harry Redknapp as Manager. The two Harry's that arrived in my life in October 2008 were most welcome!!

Sara and I sat behind the dugout at this stage of the season, even though I was well aware that she might hear language that a three year old shouldn't hear. However I was amused by what came out of our Assistant Manager David McDonald's mouth. His constant berating of the linesmen sounded even harsher in his strong Irish accent. I have never heard anyone on the touchline accuse the opposition Manager of having "little man syndrome" before or since. His constant spats were amusing to me and fortunately Sara didn't repeat what she heard. I'm not sure if it was just his touchline manners that led to him leaving the club soon afterwards.

In November, our form dropped alarmingly with six league defeats in a row as well as an early FA Trophy exit to lower league Uxbridge as well as an embarrassing 3-2 defeat to Waltham Abbey in the Isthmian League Cup having been 2-0 up. In early December the impressive striker Sean Sonnor joined the club from Northwood and his goals and work ethic had a huge bearing in Boreham Wood eventually staying up. A last minute Lee Allinson winner at home to relegation rivals Heybridge Swift at the end of January, was our first league win for nearly two months. This was followed by away draws at Maidstone and Hastings and a defeat at home to Harrow Borough. During this time we had some new arrivals including Ryan Kirby and Curtis Ujah at the back (Adedeji and Harvey had left the club by this stage). They both had a huge impact at the club. Kirby was a vastly experienced defender who would eventually become Assistant Manager. Ujah a much younger player impressed straight away. It was a shame that his time at the club came to an end following an injury the following season while on trial with Watford.

In mid-February we won 2-0 at home against Wealdstone with goals from Daly and Sonnor. It was at the game, I moved from behind the dug out to sit with Mo, Baz and Linda in the corner by the player's tunnel. So far I'd had fairly brief conversations with those around me regarding players and matches but had kept my thoughts to myself. Unfortunately three year old Sara wasn't ready to discuss our lack of goals, bad home form, poor crowds and our nosedive down the table!! Having spent the first half of the season walking Sara around the ground I'd exchanged brief words with Mo, Baz and Linda. This night I decided to take the plunge and sit with them. I have sat, stood and travelled to away games with them ever since. Although this win against Wealdstone was welcome, we went on to win only two of our last twelve games matches before the end of the season. This included a critical 1-0 win over Ashford Town (Middlesex) and an amazing 2-1 win away at runaway champions Dover Athletic with goals from Sonnor and Noto. This was their only home defeat of the whole season, the day that their stadium was packed as they received the Ryman League Trophy.

A few weeks before the Dover game, Sara and I attended our first Boreham Wood away match at Sutton United. Despite our poor form I was now beginning to have more of an affinity with the club and was genuinely concerned about relegation. I decided to take her to this game at about 1 pm on the Saturday and we missed the first ten minutes of the match. The game was awful and Sutton's 95th minute equalizer to make it 1-1 although frustrating, was well deserved. There were nearly a thousand supporters there that day but I doubted there were more than eight Boreham Wood fans amongst them.

Around this time, I was invited as a season ticket holder to a Question and Answer session with the Chairman. It was a good opportunity to meet the Chairman and other supporters, while getting an insight into the philosophy of Danny Hunter. The meeting started with Danny speaking in detail about future plans for the PASE scheme (an innovation at the club he cared passionately about) until he was rudely interrupted by some supporters who started complaining about the results on the pitch. In truth it had been a bad season but I was a bit taken aback by the blunt reaction of some of the supporters who seemed to think we should be playing in the Conference National rather than the Ryman League. Even I could see that with gates of one hundred and fifty supporters, we were lucky to still be playing in the Ryman League. I saw nothing at the club, to suggest that Conference National football was even a remote possibility. Perhaps as a new supporter, my expectations were low but we were a million miles away from Conference National level in 2009. These were the same supporters who I often heard moan a lot during matches and constantly criticize the team. Let's just say, I came away from that meeting more impressed with Danny Hunter than I was with a number of the supporters.

The victory at Dover really lifted the club. However they were brought back down to earth a few days later, losing in the last minute at home to Hendon, a shattering defeat and our thirteenth home loss of the season. Hendon had loads of supporters there that night and the noise they made, really lifted their team. We were like the away side. What a shame more locals in Borehamwood couldn't turn out for their football team. Had it been us playing at Hendon in similar circumstances we would have probably have less than a dozen supporters there.

On the penultimate Saturday of the season, Sara and I attended another away game, this time at Billericay Town. The home team took the lead just after half time and we were under the cosh for most of the game until seventeen year old Jon Clements came off the bench for us and made a significant contribution. He provided the assist for Lee Allinson to equalize with ten minutes left. The 1-1 draw was a good point ensuring that safety was in our hands going into the final Saturday of the season. If we beat Dartford at home, we were safe. We ended up drawing 0-0 with them in an entertaining match. However Margate lost at second place Staines Town, meaning Boreham Wood were a Ryman League Premier Division club once again. Margate ironically were reprieved from relegation due to King's Lynn's demise. This is a pattern and seemed to be repeated time and time again over the next few years seemingly making it very hard to actually get relegated.

My first full season as a Boreham Wood supporter was the worst of my first seven seasons watching the club. While I enjoyed the fact I was watching live football again, the team were poor and thirteen homes defeats wasn't good enough. However, at this time I still had low expectations and didn't take results to heart. There seemed to be a massive turnover of players that season with Daly, Wordsworth, Noto, Lee Allinson and Greg Morgan the only players who were still at the club from the opening day of the season. Chris Watters ended the season on loan at Staines Town but returned the following season. The best player I saw that season was Wes Daly closely followed by Wordsworth and Noto. Despite the poor entertainment and annoying supporters, I was certainly ready for more, even though I expected another battle with relegation. Like I have said, my expectations were low.

2009-2010 SEASON

You Really Got Me

I knew this was a level of football way below what I was used to watching. In the first season I hadn't expected much and the team didn't exceed these expectations. I thought the new season as going to be similar to the last. Perhaps we'd finish higher in the league, win a few more home games and even emulate the FA Trophy run of 2005-06 which everyone kept banging on about. I assumed by the end of the 2009-10 season I'd feel exactly the same about Boreham Wood FC as I'd previously done when, although I was keen to watch them and wanted them to do well, I wouldn't let bad results bother me too much. However, an awful lot changed for me during that season. I attended a lot more games both home and away and started to feel uncomfortable whenever I missed a game. Watching the team was no longer just a passing interest. I was in this for life. Also, unbeknown to me, the club was about to embark upon an amazing journey that was still going on six years later.

The summer of 2009 brought about a number of changes of personnel at the club. Unfortunately Wes Daly left for Carshalton Athletic, but fortunately all the other decent players from the previous season remained including Sonnor, Ujah, Kirby, Noto, Watters, Allinson and Morgan. Wordsworth re-signed but hardly played all season due to injury. Ujah replaced Daly as captain and Ryan Kirby was now Assistant Manager while still a player. I've often wondered whether Wes

Daly (who went on to play against us for many clubs) regretted leaving Boreham Wood in the summer of 2009. He could and should have been part of what we were about to achieve. A number of new players arrived including the excellent Tony Tucker in goal, the dependable Daniel Brathwaite at left back, Leon Hunter and Bobby Highton in midfield as well as Jamie Richards and Dean Green up front. Kevin Stephens the right back who had been on loan from Telford, signed permanently. Of all these new players, Dean Green was the only one who didn't last the season. Young homegrown players like Jon Clement and Bradley Fraser had huge impacts as the season went on, while Joe Reynolds impressed early on.

The first pre-season match took place on 9th July against Neil Warnock's Crystal Palace (arranged as part of the Simon Thomas transfer the previous season). I missed the game because I was in Cardiff watching England and Australia play cricket in the First Ashes Test. However, two days later I watched Boreham Wood lose 4-1 to an impressive Watford team with my Watford supporting brother Alex in attendance. I stubbornly missed an excellent 0-0 draw against Arsenal but watched a very good 1-0 win against Conference side Grays Athletic.

The pre-season went well and led me to believe we'd have a good start. The opening game against Hastings was no "battle" but a boring 0-0 draw, followed by three consecutive defeats. We lost away at Hornchurch and Margate as well as a feisty match at home to Wealdstone in which I arrived five minutes late and already missed the only goal of the match. As I was heading towards the exit just before the final whistle, I was witness to a very heated debate between Ian Allinson and his recently substituted son Lee. I then realised that even at Ryman League level, football was an emotional game and things can be said in the heat of the moment. I didn't quite understand why one of our supporters felt the need to make a complaint to the club about these exchange of words. If you don't want to hear bad language from the dugout, I'd suggest sitting elsewhere in the ground (or preferably outside it). This was the first of four absorbing matches that season with my former hometown club, Wealdstone.

After the match that night, I had doubts whether Ian Allinson would survive as Boreham Wood Manager. I didn't want him to go, but was unsure of the mindset of the Chairman as to whether the poor season the year before and the three successive defeats were acceptable. Clearly the results weren't good enough but to my mind we had a new team and they had to have a chance to gel properly. Following the Wealdstone defeat, things turned around with the signing of forward Sos Yao who scored in our next two games, 2-0 wins against Ashford Town (Middlesex) away and Billericay Town at home. The Billericay game stood out because we were so dominant. It was nice to see Greg Morgan get on the score sheet, as it was the first goal I'd ever seen him score. The following Saturday we won with a late Dean Green goal at Sutton United. I found out the score in the Non-League Paper on Sunday morning. This was the last time I would wait until Sunday to find out a Boreham Wood score. The following week, a late Lee Allinson goal at home to Waltham Forest in the First Qualifying Round of the FA Cup made it four wins out of four in all competitions.

In late September 2009 we played Wealdstone at home again, this time in the Second Qualifying Round of the FA Cup, a match sandwiched between two 3-1 wins against Carshalton Athletic and Horsham. The Wealdstone game stuck in the memory for many reasons. It was the first visit to Boreham Wood FC for my son Harry, not even one year old, but crawling around everywhere and making a nuisance of himself. Paula was out for the day so I was lumbered with both children at football for the first time. I hoped it would be the first of many times but also hoped it would be easier than this in future. The match was a cracker but we lost 4-2 to a very good Wealdstone side having missed a hatful of chances that would have won two football matches. As well as this match being Harry's debut watching Boreham Wood, it was also significant because I was absolutely gutted we lost. I had trouble sleeping that night, thinking about one of Leon Hunter's near misses. This is the first time I had taken a Boreham Wood defeat like this. I really fancied a good cup run. Wealdstone had a massive following that day and seemed to sing for the whole match. I'd always had a soft spot for the club being my hometown non-league club. I was aware that since becoming the first team to win "the non-league double" in 1985 (Conference and FA Trophy) they lost their ground, nearly folded following an almost suicidal ground share agreement with Watford. They wouldn't have survived but for their loyal fan base who finally looked like they were reaping the rewards for their patience and support. Having spent many years ground sharing with the likes of Edgware Town and Northwood and an aborted attempt to secure a home at the Prince Edward Playing Fields in Canons Park (now The Hive home of Barnet FC) Wealdstone now at last had their own home at the former Ruislip Manor ground Grosvenor Vale. Wealdstone were managed by Gordon Bartlett, one of my favourite characters in non-league football. At this point he had been manager there for fifteen years achieving four promotions (He was to achieve another one in 2014). If you haven't read his book "Off the Bench: A Quarter of a Century of Non-League Management", it's well worth a read.

The Wealdstone FA Cup defeat was just a blip as we won our next two matches against Horsham (away) and Bognor Regis (home). By the end of October we had knocked Waltham Abbey and Slough Town out of the FA Trophy. Summer signing Jamie Richards really started to impress up front with plenty of goals and impressive performances that led Boreham Wood to a position in the play-off places.

It was around this time, defender Curtis Ujah was being talked about in glowing terms. Since the start of the season he seemed to thrive in the captaincy role and turned in impressive performances week in week out. This form brought a lot of interest from league clubs and Championship side Watford were keen for him to play in a trial match for their reserves whose team happened to play their matches at Meadow Park. After twenty five minutes of this trial match, Ujah left the pitch due to what was described at the time as a "minor knee injury". At the Tonbridge Angels game the following Saturday word went around that he'd be out for about ten weeks. As it happened Curtis Ujah was out of the game for a year. By the time he played again he'd left Boreham Wood. It was such a shame for his Boreham Wood career to have ended like that and a disappointment for him as he never got the opportunity to show a league club what he could do again.

During this period, former Boreham Wood player Ryan Moran returned to the club to replace the stricken Curtis Ujah. Luke Garrard, AFC Wimbledon legend and full time Boreham Wood PASE coach arrived on loan. On Tuesday 10th November, Boreham Wood FC did something I'd never seen before. The club were in the middle of an FA Trophy run and had the Isthmian League Cup and Herts Senior Cup to play. To avoid an inevitable fixture pile up, they split the squad and played Royston Town in the Herts Senior Cup and (you've guessed it) Wealdstone in the Isthmian League Cup both away, on the same night. At the time it seemed like a bad idea but it turned out to be the best thing that could have happened. I attended the Wealdstone game at Grosvenor Vale. It was only two days after Wealdstone got beaten at home by League One Rotherham United in the First Round of the FA Cup. It was a bit like after the Lord Mayor's Show. The temporary stand was still up but the crowd was understandably minimal. There were four Boreham Wood supporters there that night including me and three club officials!! I assume the rest of our many hundred fans were at Royston Town instead. It was easier for the PA announcer to read the crowd changes to the players rather than the other way round. I arrived at the ground munching a Kebab when Brian Behrman (loyal Wood supporter and club official) said "Brett, you might have to go in goal as the keeper hasn't turned up". I panicked for a minute, thinking "I'm not match fit" and "the last time I went in goal I let in thirteen goals for Pinner Albion" and "can I finish my kebab first?". Perhaps I would be a hero in a penalty shootout and all the players would jump on me like they do on the television in big cup finals. Fortunately at that moment the goalkeeper James Courtnage arrived and I was spared. I then finished my Kebab and went to take my seat in the stand. I never did ask Brian if he was actually joking about me going in goal. The match itself was entertaining but unfortunately despite a great performance from Chris Watters, Wealdstone beat us for the third time that season. The Boreham Wood team at Royston Town, matched our 3-1 defeat and we were out of two cup competitions on the same night. These defeats left us to concentrate on the League and the FA Trophy. Wealdstone on the other hand were having excellent runs in all cup competitions so had the fixture pile up that we avoided. This was significant towards the end of the season because Wealdstone faded badly and I've no doubt would have made the play offs but for these distractions.

The following Saturday, Sara and I went to see my brother Elliot who lived in Kent and was about to accompany us to his first Boreham Wood match at runaway leaders Dartford. Unfortunately the heavy rain put paid to the match. This was another blessing as when we eventually played them later in the season their form had dropped off. I'm convinced we would have lost if the match has taken place on schedule. The following Tuesday we were at home to Kingstonian only to be undone by a harsh late penalty to lose 1-0. Stand in skipper Kevin Stephens ruptured his anterior cruciate ligaments and would be out for the remainder of the season. This was another crushing blow to go with the Ujah injury. Stephens would also never play for the club again. I know Curtis Ujah went on to play for other clubs at our level. I'm not sure what happened to Kevin Stephens. Midfielder Bobby Highton filled in at right back until injury ended his season in February. The increasingly impressive Mario Noto became captain.

The dual cup defeats and the injury to Stephens, led to a bad run of form in November and most of December where we registered a single victory, a 1-0 win at home to Hungerford Town in the Third Qualifying round of the FA Trophy. We were drawn away to Conference National high-flyers AFC Wimbledon in the Fourth Qualifying round on 12th December. AFC Wimbledon was born out of the ashes of the old Wimbledon FC who relocated to Milton Keynes in 2002. The club literally started again and rose through the leagues having been promoted to the Conference National in 2009. (They were to achieve Football League status in 2011). By 2009 Wimbledon were an impressive outfit with Jon Main and Danny Kedwell scoring goals for fun. They went on to finish just outside the play off places. Despite their pedigree, AFC Wimbledon has never actually beaten Boreham Wood in four previous meetings. This fixture was an eye opener for me because it was my first big game. Sara and I went on a coach with Mo, Baz and Linda as well as a number of other Boreham Wood supporters. The match was segregated and we stood behind the goal. There were plenty of other people supporting Boreham Wood who I'd never seen in a season and a half. Every club has them, those who only turn up for big games. There was a lot of singing and a good atmosphere. Leon Hunter gave Boreham Wood the lead midway through the second half but unfortunately two late goals sealed the tie for Wimbledon. I was gutted but we gave a good account of ourselves and I felt deserved at least a replay.

On Boxing Day 2009, we won their first league game in two months with a comfortable 3-0 win at home to Waltham Abbey. Following this win there was an enforced three week break due to bad weather meaning a number of matches were postponed. This break actually did us some good because it gave the squad a useful mid-season break to regroup. During this time, they had the artificial pitch to continue training on while other clubs who used more traditional methods couldn't train properly. This was a distinct advantage to us when we resumed playing. By this stage of the season there had been a few changes in personnel. Forwards Sos Yao and Dean Green left the club while Sean Sonnor having failed to reproduce the form of the previous season, joined Slough Town. Luke Garrard who was previous on loan from Wim-bledon rejoined Boreham Wood permanently in February. Just before the Boxing Day clash, centre half Ryan Kirby picked up an injury, giving a debut to seventeen year old Bradley Fraser who partnered Ryan Moran in defence. Fra-ser impressed straight away and held onto his place for the remainder of the season.

After the enforced break, Boreham Wood resumed their league season on a Monday night in mid-January with an impressive 2-0 win at Tooting & Micham followed by a narrow 3-2 win at home to Aveley. The following Saturday, my brother Elliot and my nephew Finn joined me and Sara for an away trip to watch Boreham Wood play Maidstone United (at Ashford in Kent where they played home games). The pitch clearly hadn't recovered from the bad weather. Half of it was caked in mud while the rest of it was extremely soggy. Our only centre forward Jamie Richards was unavailable that day so eighteen year old PASE striker Inih Effiong made his debut up front. There is no doubt Effiong divided opinion while playing for Boreham Wood but he was outstanding that day. The team was excellent too with the exceptional Mario Noto scoring the winner from the penalty spot . Jon Clements who impressed me so much when coming off the bench at Billericay the previous season, made his first start of the season. The Maidstone result and performance gave me as much satisfaction as any result this season.

Take Me I'm Yours

The following Tuesday night, I had to choose between Boreham Wood and Spurs. Tottenham were live on Sky against Fulham while Boreham Wood entertained Aveley at home. In truth there was only one winner. The way Boreham Wood had played at Maidstone and the run they were on, meant I didn't want to miss the Aveley game. The 3-2 win was our fourth in a row in the league. Having missed the Tooting & Mitcham match in mid-January, I only missed a further two of the last twenty four games that season. I was now hooked and there was no going back.

We secured our fifth win in a row the following Saturday with a dominant 4-0 victory at home to Horsham with Jamie Richards scoring a fantastic header following some great build up play. Chris Watters scored a cracker from outside the box in the final minute. This was the best performance I'd seen from a Boreham Wood team that season. Unfortunately this was the end of our winning run as successive home defeats against Canvey Island and Cray Wanderers followed. By mid-February we were back on track with a 2-1 home win, coming from behind to beat Hendon at home. An excellent Greg Morgan header sealed a 1-0 win away at Bognor Regis the following week. The club laid on a minibus to West Sussex that day.

The matches were coming thick and fast but our form dipped again, losing our next three games, at home to Dartford and Sutton United and away at Kingstonian. The Kingstonian match took place on a Sunday and it was our "day of rest" in front of goal as we missed a hatful of clear cut chances in 4-1 defeat. It was our second visit of the season to their ground having played landlords AFC Wimbledon in December. My brother Alex and my nephew Oz (who live in Richmond) joined me and Sara for that match whilst the women and one year old Harry went shopping in Kingston. We were more impressed with the Kingsmeadow bar then match. Despite these three defeats, we were still lurking in and around the play off positions.

I missed the Harrow Borough home game on Saturday 13th March as I had a long standing arrangement to take Paula away for a long weekend in the Peak District. While we were touring the Bakewell Pudding Factory in Derbyshire (munching away at all the samples) Greg Morgan scored the only goal in a much needed 1-0 win. I arrived back home on the Monday, in time for the rearranged match away to Dartford on the Tuesday night. Again, a minibus was on hand to take away supporters and again I coerced one of my brothers to come to the match. This time Elliot joined me, having left his Partners meeting at work early to attend an "important meeting in Dartford". This match gave us an indication of how much the team had improved and settled down after a devastating run of injuries. Goalkeeper Tony Tucker was immense. Ryan Moran and young Bradley Fraser almost faultless at the back. Noto was dominant in midfield and Jamie Richards was playing the loan striker role impressively while Morgan and Watters continued their great form on the wings. Another wide player, Dwayne Clarke joined from Harrow Borough in time for the Dartford game and went straight into the side to replace Chris Watters who needed a rest. Our performance against Dartford mirrors many we produced over the next few weeks. We were a little under pressure in the first half but our defence stood up to the test. A great header from Ryan Moran just before half time gave us the lead. Dartford equalized early in the second half only for Greg Morgan to score an excellent winner a few minutes later.

I firmly believed after the Dartford game, that we would get in the play offs. The team seemed to have a buzz about it. Surely another victory at Aveley the following Saturday would help cement this. The grounds at Dartford and Aveley couldn't have been more different. Dartford was an impressive purpose built stadium with a good pitch and an excellent bar while Aveley's Mill Field ground looked like it hadn't had a lick of paint for years, the wooden stand was a wreck, the bar looked like a disused scout hut. Unfortunately the performance of the Boreham Wood team mirrored this contrast. We were a shadow of a team that day and it was almost as if the result at Dartford sapped all our energy. My brother Elliot, full of enthusiasm from the Tuesday night, came to the match. The performance was probably the worst of the season not helped by Jamie Richards, our only recognized striker getting a straight red card in the first half with a subsequent three match ban. The 2-0 defeat flattered us. I remember thinking as I left the ground, "I'm pleased we won't have to play here again in a hurry". The irony is, the match was free to get in for all supporters. I still felt ripped off.

The Final Countdown

After the Aveley defeat we had two draws against Waltham Abbey (away) and Margate (home), both games which we should have won. Dwayne Clarke started a three match ban for a sending off he received at Harrow Borough before joining us and Jamie Richards was also banned. This hit our depleted squad very hard. We couldn't rely on youngster Inih Effiong as our only striker. He showed plenty of promise but hadn't scored yet.

Before the Canvey Island match away on 3rd April, the club made a signing that solved our goalscoring problem and eventually led us to promotion. Former Spurs and Watford youngster Claude Seanla arrived from Horsham to add some much needed firepower. I nearly missed the Canvey Island match as Sara didn't want to go. Paula didn't want me to take Harry and she felt it was unfair for me to clear off without them for the whole afternoon. Fortunately, following my moaning and groaning, Paula arranged to see a friend last minute with the kids, leaving me free to attend. I arrived at the ground early to watch most of the Manchester United v Chelsea match in the bar which prove to be a Premier League title decider (Chelsea won the match and eventually the title). I had a nice chat with Wealdstone manager Gordon Bartlett who was there to watch Boreham Wood (in preparation for our forthcoming fixture) as his team's match was called off. The match itself was significant because it was the start of an unbeaten run for the final six league games and two play-off matches. We only conceded two goals in the process. This match was a tight affair with an excellent debut goal by Seanla winning it for Boreham Wood. There was nothing the young Canvey Island goalkeeper could do about Seanla's finish but he made a couple of good saves. We were speaking to him during the match from behind the goal and he came across as a nice chap despite his team's plight. At final whistle, he wished us good luck in the play offs, a confident statement as we had a lot to do and we weren't there yet. The Canvey Island goalkeeper's name was James Russell.

The following Tuesday night we were away at Hendon (at Wembley FC where they were playing home games at the time). My friend Pervez and his girlfriend Emily who lived locally joined us for the match. The opening exchanges of the match were memorable because as we were making our way behind the goal, poor old Emily carrying her hot chocolate was hit by the ball following a stray shot, spilling her drink all over her lovely white coat. Fortunately she saw the funny side of it while giving the rest of us a good laugh. We were excellent that night and probably should have won by more than the second half Mario Noto penalty. Wealdstone Manager Gordon Bartlett was there again and even commented in his book about how strong the Boreham Wood team was starting to look. Pervez and Emily enjoyed the match and the drinks in the bar afterwards, especially as we were invited to finished off the sandwiches, sausage rolls and scotch eggs that the players didn't eat. They said they would come to watch Boreham Wood again but haven't been since. Perhaps Emily didn't want to spend any more money on dry cleaning!

The following Saturday marked the start of a very busy week for my two football teams, Boreham Wood and Spurs. On the Saturday we played Wealdstone for the fourth time this season. Although they beat us three times already, things were different now. Boreham Wood were a different team to the one who rolled over against them earlier in the season. Wealdstone on the other hand were running on empty having played plenty of cup matches. As well as this, the bad weather meant that they were playing catch up in the league and were now outside the play off places. We were in the last play-off spot at this stage. I fully expected us to beat them so was left disappointed with a 0-0 draw although we played well again. After the match my attention was drawn to the forthcoming FA Cup Semi-Fnal where Spurs were to play Portsmouth at Wembley the following day. Having lost our last four semi-finals in the Cup I fully expected us to beat Pompey with plenty to spare. Spurs were doing well under Harry Redknapp and heading for the Champions League. Portsmouth on the other hand were virtually bankrupt and heading for relegation from the Premier League. With that in mind Spurs's 2-0 defeat after extra time was heartbreaking. Since our glorious 1991 Semi Final win against Arsenal at Wembley, Spurs had now lost five FA Cup Semi Final's in a row. With that in mind Tottenham were about to go into the North London Derby against Arsenal on the Wednesday night, having not beaten them in the league for eleven years. The contrast from the Sunday to the Wednesday mirrored the Dartford and Aveley games. Spurs beat Arsenal 2-1 with the "goal of the season" by young Danny Rose and a second from Gareth Bale who was starting to show what he could do. *Heurelho Gomes produced one of the best goalkeeping displays I've ever seen to keep Arsenal out* and maintain our push for a Champions League spot. Spurs followed this up with a similar 2-1 win the following Saturday at home against Chelsea with the improving Gareth Bale scoring again.

On the penultimate Saturday of the League season, Boreham Wood had a tricky encounter at Tonbridge Angels. Tonbridge had gone on an amazing run of form, winning ten and drawing two of their last twelve league matches and were level on points with Boreham Wood competing for a play-off place. Unfortunately I missed the match as we had a long standing arrangement with another family that I couldn't get out of. This was the first game I'd missed since 6th February at Carshalton and, as you might expect, by 3pm I was a nervous wreck. Soon afterwards, the other dad and I took the kids to the park and while pushing Harry on the swings with one hand I was trying to find out the score from my mobile phone with the other. On reflection I probably came across a bit rude to the other dad. He was trying to engage in conversation and I wasn't having any of it. These were in the early days of the "smart phone" and I was already having doubts about my recently purchased HTC device. I remember looking on the BBC App just after the away match at Maidstone in January to see the astonishing scoreline "Manchester United 0 Hull City 4". United were an excellent team in early 2010 while Hull were near the bottom of the Premier League, so the scoreline was a shock. However I quickly realised after turning the radio on in the car that it was actually 4-0 to United. In those days I thought "tweeting" was something that birds did, there was no information on Facebook and Boreham Wood FC didn't even have their own proper website. Unfortunately the Ryman League scores weren't a high priority on the BBC website. I managed to find the Non-League Vidiprinter but again, there was nothing on the Ryman League scores. With twenty minutes left of play, I still didn't know the score even though other Ryman League score updates started to come through. All of a sudden the score flashed up as "Tonbridge Angels 0 Boreham Wood 2 – Noto 65, Seanla 69". I jumped up and down in a busy park with lots of people looking at me. I didn't care as it appeared we'd come through a real challenge with flying colours. I assume those in the park that afternoon, still talk about the day the large bloke with a shaved head starting jumping up and down screaming "yeeeees" while holding a mobile phone and pushing a toddler on the swings. The score ended 2-0 and with one match to go Boreham Wood and Wealdstone were both on sixty five points but our goal different was +6 more than them. Basically we had to equal or better Wealdstone's result on the final day of the league season to make the play offs.

On the final day, we were at home to Tooting & Mitcham while Wealdstone entertained Carshalton. I fully expected both teams to win especially as Carshalton were in a dogfight towards the bottom of the table. Our fears were eased quite early on as by the half hour mark Wealdstone were already 4-0 down. A hat trick by ex Boreham Wood player Byron Harrison ensured Gordon Bartlett's men would be playing Ryman League football again the following season. Boreham Wood on the other hand started the Tooting match well and Mario Noto's twenty five yard volley after fifteen minutes brought scenes of wild celebration. Noto doubled the advantage four minutes later to make it 2-0. Unfortunately we took our foot off the gas and two well worked goals by Tooting and Mitcham made it 2-2 at half time. These were the only two goals we conceded in our final eight matches and we were panicking a little bit. Fortunately a fantastic lob by Claude Seanla gave us a 3-2 victory and secured a play-off spot. Seanla was later given a straight red card and would be banned for the first three games of the following season. At the final whistle, it emerged that Kingstonian only drew at home to Maidstone United so we ended up above them in fourth place. This would prove crucial over the next week. The Play Off Semi Finals at this level was a single tie played in midweek at the home of the team who finished higher in the league. The final would be the following Saturday between the two semi-final winners, again at the home of the highest placed team. This meant another trip to Aveley (who finished third) on Monday night, a trip to a ground I'd hoped not to go to again.

Although the supporters were happy celebrating making the play offs, Ian Allinson and the squad took a more measured approach and correctly analysed that there was nothing to actually celebrate. We were in the play offs but it meant nothing if we couldn't finish the job. On the Monday morning I bought the Non-League Paper and saw to my amazement a picture of the Aveley team popping the champagne corks and presumably spraying each other with the contents. I couldn't believe my eyes. They looked like they were celebrating not only reaching the play offs but the Premier League title, the Champions League and even the Grand National. Aveley like Tonbridge beforehand were in cracking form, winning nine of their last twelve games having played ten of those games in the last twenty one days due to a fixture pile up. I know getting to the play offs was a great achievement for a little club in the wilds of Essex but it was also an achievement for Boreham Wood. In my opinion, at this point the match was won. The Aveley players had given Boreham Wood's team talk for them. Ian Allinson's job was done for him. I wouldn't have expected a Manager like Aveley's Rod Stringer to let his players get so carried away at this stage. Stringer performed miracles there and would prove a very successful manager at Braintree and Bishops Stortford over the next few years. This apparent "premature celebration" from Aveley had happened before. In the 1968-69 season in the Athenian League Division Two, Aveley were ahead of Boreham Wood and thought they'd won the league but an unbeaten run gave the title to

Boreham Wood on goal difference under Manager Mickey Hunter.

The match was a cagey affair with few chances. Aveley perhaps had the better of the first half with a good chance that Tucker saved well. It was clear that the match was going to be settled by one goal and the way our defence was playing it wasn't us who would concede it. On seventy nine minutes, a Lee Allinson corner was powerfully headed in the corner of the net by Claude Seanla to notch his fourth goal in seven matches since joining Boreham Wood, three of them winners. The Boreham Wood supporters went berserk and the last eleven minutes seemed to go relatively quickly with Morgan replacing Dwayne Clark to add some fresh legs. The final whistle blew and Boreham Wood were in the Play-Off Final to face either Sutton United or Kingstonian who played the following evening at Sutton.

During a discussion with my boss the following day, it occurred to me that we might still have home advantage in the Final. If Kingstonian beat Sutton that night we would play them at home as we'd finished above them in the league. Bear in mind we always seemed to be chasing the last play-off spot; I'd always assumed we'd be playing away in the Final. With that in mind, I obviously wanted a Kingstonian win. However, I didn't think this was possible as Sutton were an impressive side and would surely overcome what I thought was a pretty poor Kingstonian side. That evening I had a romantic night in with Paula. She was ironing and I was pressing the refresh button on the non-league website. Sutton led 2-1 at half time so I checked the train timetable to Sutton and realised the direct train from Boreham Wood to West Sutton (right next to the ground) wasn't running due to engineering works. Perhaps the club would lay on a minibus again. The second half started and my finger was still hitting the refresh button. After fifty minutes it was 2-2. After sixty three minutes, twenty eight goal top scorer Bobby Traynor made it 3-2 to Kingstonian. I cheered loudly causing a stern rebuff from Paula. "You'll wake the kids up". After seventy four minutes, Traynor scored again to make it 4-2 and ended the tie as a contest. Kingstonian had won against the odds at Sutton, giving Boreham Wood home advantage against them in the final, five days later. Everything seemed to be going our way. This is probably the last time I ever wanted Kingstonian to win a match.

All or Nothing

Although the five days between the Sutton Vs Kingstonian match and the Play off Final was extremely nerve wracking, I was very confident we would win. The simple fact is, we weren't letting in any goals and with Claude Seanla up front we could always score one. Even though Kingstonian had done the double over us in the league I didn't rate them. I woke up that Saturday morning after my fifth interrupted sleep in a row and was pretty sure we would be celebrating today. In order to go to the Play off Final I missed a family tea at my Uncle and Aunt's. Sara was given the choice between coming to the match and going there. I was disappointed she chose not to come to the match as she'd have enjoyed the occasion. She was only four years old and didn't understand the significance of the game.

As for the match itself, Boreham Wood lining up, Tucker, Garrard, Brathwaite, Moran, Fraser, Clements, Allinson, Noto, Watters, Clarke and Seanla which seemed to be a pretty stable team for the last few weeks. Leon Hunter had been injured and replaced by the excellent Clements. Jamie Richards was on hand to come on if we needed a goal and Greg Morgan could come on if we needed someone to hold the ball up to see out time. Despite the occasion, the 1,100 crowd were treated to a very entertaining match with both teams interested in playing football. The score was 0-0 at half time and the match controversially exploded into life in the fiftieth minute when Kingstonian Captain Francis Duku was punched by a Boreham Wood "supporter" who entered the field of play. From the other end this was shocking to see and clearly has no place in football. The "supporter" was taken out of the ground and presumably arrested. There has rightly been a lot of condemnation about this incident since but I was convinced Duku was about to be sent off by the referee just before he was punched. The game carried on and after sixty nine minutes, Boreham Wood were awarded a free kick to the right hand side of the penalty area. Up steps Lee Allinson to take it and up pops Ryan Moran to bury the header at the far post, a fantastic header by this outstanding centre half to give Boreham Wood a 1-0 lead, a goal that his brilliant performance deserved. This Boreham Wood team who had got out of the habit of letting in goals had just twenty one minutes to hold out and Conference South football would be theirs. During that time Kingstonian made two substitutions and their "stricken" captain Frances Duku remained on the pitch. Tony Tucker made an outstanding save with ten minutes left and was about to end the season with twenty three clean sheets. No other goalkeeper in the top seven divisions of English Football could match this amount of clean sheets throughout this season. As the clock ticked down, Boreham Wood were holding out well and we made our way to the front of the stand for the rush onto the pitch. At that point the ball was played from the back to Mario Noto who had been such a colossus in midfield. He played a nicely weighted pass to the right to Dwayne Clarke who presumably was going to hold the ball up in the corner. Instead of that, Clarke took a touch and hit an unbelievable shot across the Kingstonian goalkeeper into the top corner of the net, definitely the best goal we'd scored all season and a nice way to wrap up a 2-0 win and promotion with two minutes left on the clock. The full time whistle went and we made our way onto the "hallowed turf" to celebrate with other supporters and players. The atmosphere at this stage was incredible. Mario Noto lifted the trophy and everyone was delighted. At this point it started raining and I made my way out of the ground (via a hug with the Chairman) to join the rest of the family at my Uncle and Aunt's in Elstree.

There was a slight spanner in the works a couple of days later when Kingstonian, despite gracefully accepting defeat after the match, appealed the result due to the incident with the "Boreham Wood supporter" and Frances Duku. Although the incident was disgraceful, Duku remained on the pitch despite Kingstonian making two substitutions. Surely if what happened had affected him he'd have come off. Despite this I was beginning to doubt that we would take our place in the Conference South for no other reason than that I was being negative. I even wrote to the club voicing my concerns. At it happened, I needn't have worried because Kingstonian's appeal was unsuccessful and rightly Boreham Wood correctly took their place in the sixth tier of English football. I thought the way Kingstonian tried to manipulate the situation was a disgrace and I'm pleased that five years later they remained in the Ryman League no doubt still bitter about what might have been.

Celebration

I'm not sure why it happened but some genius at the club decided to hold the "End of Season Presentation Night" after the Play off Final rather than its traditional place on the last

Saturday of the league season. When it was booked, we can't have known we'd be in the Play-off Final. I decided long ago to attend my first Presentation Night. The event was held at The Holiday Inn (formerly The Moat House). Over the years, I have always found these occasions great fun, with plenty of food, drink and amusing conversation. It's always good to speak to the players as well. Quite often throughout the season the only conversation you would have with the players is to wish them "good luck" before a game or to say "well done" or "unlucky" afterwards or give them one of those raised "high fives". This action is a cross between a normal high five and a hand shake and it seems to have been patented by non-league footballers as I've never seen anyone else do it.

Having returned from my Uncle and Aunt's house, I quickly got changed into my suit and went to the Holiday Inn all set for a night of celebrating. Not many supporters attended which surprised me. I bet more wish they were there. Apart from club officials, Linda, John Weston and I were the only supporters present. I don't remember a great detail about the dinner but I did drink quite a lot during it. I started the precedent of finishing someone's dinner which I proceeded to do every year. I was like a human dustbin / hoover. For some reason, I always get put on a table where someone couldn't make it, wasn't hungry or didn't like their dessert. All this alcohol makes me hungry (like I need an excuse). Fortunately I avoided spilling gravy on my nice white shirt.

After dinner the speeches and award presentation started. Danny Hunter gave an excellent speech about what we'd achieved today and what the club was achieving overall. I felt really proud to be associated with this football club and I must admit, had a slight tear in my eye. There were a number of awards given out, most notable Tony Tucker the goalkeeper winning a well-deserved Player of the Year award. As the awards were being given out, the Chairman said "and now to the Supporter of the Year Award. This year it goes to someone who is regularly seen at football grounds across the South East with his young daughter". At this point I thought "Blimey. That's me!!" I was in total shock. I had no idea there was a Supporter of the Year Award. I quickly straightened my tie and put my suit jacket back on before the Chairman mentioned my name so I was able to walk up to the stage and collect my trophy straight away. As I walked up to collect my trophy, I passed some of the player's tables where I remember Chris Watters, Mario Noto and Luke Garrard saying "Well done Brett". After what they'd just achieved I couldn't believe they were saying well done to me. I had an official photo with Manager Ian Allinson and the trophy and then sat back down again to widespread congratulations from everyone on my table. I had a big smile on my face for the rest of the night. In thirty years as a Spurs fan no one has ever given me an award for going to loads of games or even acknowledged my support. The rest of the night was mixed with drinking beer, wine and scotch while talking to players and various other people present. Fortunately I don't think I made a fool of myself. The last thing I remember of the night was sitting in the bar of the hotel at 3:30am with the Chairman and the Manager drinking beer. I somehow made my way home and fortunately the Supporter of the Year trophy was still intact. After I got home, I turned on the computer, logged into Facebook and typed in capital letters "WE ARE GOING UP. WE ARE GOING UP".

What a night, what a day, what a season!!

Boreham Wood's rather athletic looking bench. Bishop's Stortford away in 2011

Sara is in need of a bit of Dutch courage before Bromley away in 2011

2010-2011 SEASON

Who Are You

Following the euphoria of the Play off Final win and promotion to the Conference South, came what seemed like a very long break. The week after the Kingstonian victory while the "Ks" were appealing the result, those at Boreham Wood FC saw no reason to be concerned. The players and many of the staff went on a well-earned break to Puerto Banus, while Tottenham qualified for the Champions League for the first time in their history and the nation elected the first coalition government since World War Two. During this break, we had the World Cup to look forward to in South Africa and hopefully news of some quality signings for Boreham Wood. Unfortunately both turned out to be uninspiring.

In terms of player turnover, unfortunately goalkeeper Tony Tucker left the club. From my understanding he was unable to combine his full time job with the extra travel required as a Conference South player. Living in the wilds of Essex, it was hard for him to even commit to training. This is a problem a number of players at this level have, something perhaps supporters don't understand. The contribution Tucker made to our promotion was immense and he'll always be a Boreham Wood legend. I also don't remember a player who was so hard to replace. Another big loss was Jon Clement who had been exceptional on the run in. He'd accepted a scholarship to study and play in the US, a great opportunity for him but bad timing for us. Also out of the door were Chris Watters, Leon

Hunter and Jamie Richards who'd contributed enormously to our promotion. Inih Effiong left the club for local rivals St Albans. New arrivals included former AFC Wimbledon midfielder Elliot Godfrey, Sherwin Stanley from Aveley and prolific goal scorer Stuart Blackburne from Enfield Town. Goalkeeper Simon Overland returned to the club as a replacement for Tony Tucker but was surprisingly released after the first two pre-season games. Gareth Williams replaced him between the sticks before the start of the season. Stanley and Blackburne didn't stay beyond the first few league fixtures. Godfrey was the only summer signing who was still at the club by the end of the season. The rest of the players from the previous campaign remained including Claude Seanla and Dwayne Clarke. It was clear that Allinson wanted to give most of those who had got us promotion the chance to keep us up.

Our first pre-season match against Dagenham & Redbridge was on the same day as Spain beat Germany in the World Cup semi-final ensuring a low crowd. This is just as well as we lost 4-0 and played poorly. A young player called Graeme Montgomery was playing for Dagenham that night. This was followed up by a 5-0 thrashing by Watford the following Saturday. A week later we played well and were unlucky not to beat Championship side QPR who relied on a late equalizer to secure a 1-1 draw. I missed the rest of pre-season because I went on holiday to Spain with the family. I did plan to go to the Arsenal pre-season match this year but was eating paella and drinking sangria at the time.

When the fixtures were released, they threw up a very interesting first match for Boreham Wood as a Conference South club. We were to play Weston Super Mare away. This reminded me of school as my classmates always seemed to go there on holiday. This was a bit of a trek for our first game but I was keen to go so took Sara, Mo, Baz and Linda in my car. Our turnout was poor. Despite promotion, there was still little interest in our club from the town and only a handful of supporters were there that day. Weston Super Mare had a new manager and ten new players in their starting line-up so we had a perfect opportunity to get off to a good start in Somerset. Blackburne and Stanley made their debuts up front while James Hawes was covering for the injured Brathwaite at left back. Claude Seanla was suspended for the first three matches and Dwayne Clarke was on holiday. We appeared to have lost the zip of the previous campaign and Weston were probably no better than some of the teams we'd beaten at the back end of the previous campaign. The match was pretty poor and it was obvious that whoever scored first would win but in truth it had 0-0 written all over it. Just before the hour mark James Hawes was sent off and on seventy-two minutes a mix up between Gareth Williams and Bradley Fraser led to the opening goal from Weston. They sealed a 2-0 win with a penalty right at the end.

We lost again the following Tuesday night at home to Bromley 4-2 in a much more entertaining game despite the heaviest rain I've ever seen at a football match. Had it been raining an hour earlier I'm sure the match would have been postponed. It was Mario Noto's turn to be sent off that night. The following Saturday we got our first point in an entertaining 2-2 draw with Thurrock, a match we should have won. New signing Lee Kersey replaced Bradley Fraser in the starting line-up to add another experienced head alongside Ryan Moran at the back. Two well taken goals by Elliot Godfrey were encouraging. Towards the end there was an amusing moment when a Thurrock player got sent off for a heavy tackle on Mario Noto right in front of us and one of our overzealous supporters arranged to have a fight with him in the car park while exchanging language you wouldn't find in the House of Commons. Fortunately the fight didn't happen. The following Tuesday we played away at eventual champions Braintree now managed by last season's Aveley boss Rod Stringer. Again we played well but lost 3-2 despite an excellent team goal finished by Godfrey and the return of Seanla and Clarke to the starting line-up. Having let in eleven goals in our first four games, the following two 0-0 draws against Woking and Staines were encouraging. A brilliant strike from James Hawes gave us a half time lead against Welling United, but they turned us over 3-1 when it could have been more.

By the time we got to the Bishop's Stortford home game the following Saturday, keeper Gareth Williams was released. The apparently impressive Ashlee Jones replaced him. By this time Tony Tucker was now playing for Maldon & Tiptree, two divisions down (what a waste). Striker Leon Mackenzie also joined to add some much needed firepower to our ranks. Unfortunately it was a sign of things to come for Ashlee Jones during the Stortford match when his howler gifted them a 2-1 win despite us playing well. Defeat at Dorchester was followed by our first win of the season, at Bedford Town in the Second Qualifying Round of the FA Cup. By this time Dwayne Clarke and Claude Seanla left the club, both shadows of the players that were so outstanding towards the end of the previous season. On 2nd October we finally won our first league match at Conference South level at the tenth attempt with a masterclass performance from Mario Noto in a well-deserved 3-1 win at home to Dartford. It wasn't the last Dartford would see of Noto before the end of the season. Our third win in a row in all competitions occurred the following Saturday at home to local rivals Enfield Town in the Third Qualifying Round of the FA Cup. An entertaining match was settled in the last ten minutes by goals from Joe Benjamin and Lee Allinson in a 3-1 win. Lee Allinson's excellent chip for the third goal was his last contribution for the club as he soon left for Arlesey Town. He made a significant contribution to help get the club promoted but although a good player wasn't quite at the level required in the Conference South. In recent weeks he had often been on the bench so naturally wanted regular first team football He went on to be very successful at Arlesey and eventually Biggleswade Town winning further promotions at both clubs. We would see plenty more of Lee Allinson around the club attending matches in support of his father.

Unfortunately those three victories were a false dawn. The following Saturday's defeat at home to Ebbsfleet United was the closest thing to a 1-0 thrashing I can remember. Leon Mackenzie was sent off for us. The following week we played Ebbsfleet again, this time in the FA Cup Fourth Qualifying round away from home. We got thrashed again and Leon Mackenzie picked up his second straight red card in a row. Not surprisingly his days were numbered and he left the club. Another heavy defeat the following week at Eastleigh left Boreham Wood second from bottom and struggling badly. However there was a slight glimmer of hope at Eastleigh as the impressive Sam Hurrell made his Wood debut on a one month loan deal from Woking. A week later, he impressed again scoring in a 2-2 draw at home to Hampton & Richmond.

At this time, there were significant changes of personnel at the club. Ryan Kirby stepped down as Assistant Manager to manage the reserves. Replacing him was Jason Goodliffe who was something of a non-league legend, having plied his trade at AFC Wimbledon, Stevenage and Sutton United over the years. This was his first coaching role since retiring from playing in the summer. Forward Ali Chabaan and full back Michael Kamara also joined in time for the Hampton & Richmond match as did centre half Luke Wilkinson, on loan from Dagenham & Redbridge for the rest of the season. Hard working midfielder Gareth Risbridger joined from Staines in time for the Dover Athletic match a week later.

On Saturday 13th November we entertained Dover at Meadow Park and it was probably our best display of the season to date. Our new signings all seeming like they'd played for the club for years. Two stunning individual goals by Sam Hurrell gave us a well-deserved 2-1 lead but another howler by goalie Ashlee Jones contributed to a 3-2 defeat. This was particularly hard to take as we'd played so well. By this time I was amazed that Jones was still in the team as he seemed to undo all our good work on a weekly basis. Over the years, Boreham Wood had had a number of goalkeepers and Ian Allinson had always been quick to change them if they weren't up to scratch. I certainly felt it was time for another change in goalkeeper at this time. I'm familiar with the saying "form is temporary, class is permanent". With Jones, class was also temporary. A week after the Dover defeat we brushed aside Romford 3-0 in the Third Qualifying round of the FA Trophy.

Due to the poor winter weather, we only managed three matches in December, the first of which was only our second league win of the season at home to Weston Super Mare on a cold Wednesday evening. By this time Sam Hurrell returned to Woking when they realised what sort of player they had! Former Barnet wide man Nicky Nicolau replaced Hurrell in time for the Weston match. We were two goals down in the first seven minutes but a brace from debutant Nicolau contributed to an entertaining 6-3 win. During the match, left back Daniel Brathwaithe sustained a nasty facial injury and would be out for several weeks. Nicolau reverted to left back in time for our trip to Conference National side Eastbourne Borough in the First Round of the FA Trophy the following Saturday. Mo, Barry and I made our way to Eastbourne which was a bit of an eye opener. The club couldn't have been more stereotypical if it tried. The three of us seemed to be the youngest there by a mile, bear in mind Mo was in his mid-sixties at the time. It was the first time I'd ever seen a full size bowling green in the clubhouse and the elderly lady behind the bar took about ten minutes to give me my ten pence change having tried to work out the amount in her head. Despite Justin Cochrane's opener for us, we lost 3-1 but had played well against Conference National opposition. The following Wednesday, a late Ali Chabaan strike secured a 1-1 draw at Maidenhead. We now had to embark on a busy Christmas period.

This is the Low

Unfortunately due to the bad weather, the busy Christmas period didn't happen. The snow was playing havoc with the fixtures. It was a shame that the eagerly awaited derby against St Albans on Boxing Day fell foul of the weather. It was even more of a shame that the return fixture on New Year's Day did go ahead. The match had added significance as St Albans were bottom of the table and we were just above them. New Year's Eve is often seen as a big party night where friends or family get together to drink a lot and see in the New Year in style. It didn't disappoint as we had a cracking night at friends of ours. While the beer and wine were flowing I had one eye on the St Albans match the following day and was rather excited about my first Boreham Wood v St Albans derby. I remember trying to convince others to come with me. Thank God no one did. The following morning, Sara decided she didn't want to come to the match. Perhaps she knew what was coming.

The 3-0 defeat against St Albans on New Year's Day 2011 was definitely the worst and most embarrassing performance in my first seven years of watching Boreham Wood. I couldn't even blame goalie Ashlee Jones, because without him it would have been seven or eight. The writing was on the wall before the match when Elliot Godfrey got injured in the warm up leaving Ali Chabaan alone up front. It was former Boreham Wood player Inih Effiong who was the catalyst for our misery with two stunning goals. We were all thinking "Why didn't he do that for us?" Why did we let him go?". While there were no goals in the second half there was a lot of bickering going on among Boreham Wood supporters about the future of Ian Allinson. I appeared to be one of the only supporters who wanted him to remain as Manager. Despite our poor form since promotion I genuinely felt that having got us promoted, he deserved the right to try and keep us up. I'm sure in hindsight, discussing the fate of our manager during a 3-0 defeat against our local rivals was going to bring a knee jerk response. We were now bottom of the table.

The best thing to do after a day like New Year's Day 2011 is to put it right as soon as possible. Fortunately we only had to wait two days until our next match away at Woking which I didn't attend. Unfortunately the hangover from the St Albans defeat continued and appalling defending contributed to another 3-0 defeat with Sam Hurrell inevitably scoring for Woking. Fortunately Jon Clements who impressed so much at the end of the previous season, had returned from the United States for a few weeks and would be available for the next few fixtures. Even he couldn't turn the tide against Woking. Next up was another away game at mid table Bishops Stortford. This was slightly better. We only lost 2-0 and again were poor. My biggest memory of the Stortford match was a two year old Harry pointing constantly at the planes flying to and from Stansted Airport from his pushchair. A word of advice, if you're going to take a two year old to such an appalling match, make sure it's one that has an airport nearby so he can watch the planes. It looked like we were heading for the drop. With only eleven points from nineteen matches we were in big trouble and it didn't look like there was a way out.

Fortunately an "easy" Herts Senior Cup match at Hertford Town the following Tuesday should lift the gloom to a certain extent. I remember thinking that if we could thrash Hertford 5-0, the old confidence should come rushing back. Jason Goodliffe took charge of the team that night as Ian Allinson was otherwise engaged. To the half a dozen Wood supporters there that night (four of whom arriving in Mo's car) that was an ominous sign. However we were assured by club officials that our suspicions weren't true and there were things going on behind the scenes at the club including work to get some decent new signings on board. The match itself started well for us with Risbridger opened the scoring. However two Hertford goals sealed a 2-1 win for the home team. There are three things I remember about that night.

1) Ossie Ardiles son Pablo was playing for Hertford,

2) The catering was among the best I've have sampled at non-league level. The burger and chips were fantastic. The catering staff, all volunteers, were also really friendly.

3) We were in the shit, if we couldn't even beat Hertford Town who were several divisions below us. I hoped these new signings were good and capable of making an impact.

Calling "Elvijs"

The goings on behind the scenes during that period and the new players brought in amazingly led to our "great escape" ensuring we stayed up with something to spare. This didn't look possible in early January 2011 and I've got to give Chairman Danny Hunter credit here. He could have quite easily panicked and sacked Ian Allinson bringing in a new manager and hope for the best. Instead of that he backed the Gaffer, brought in some new players and got rid of ineffective ones. One of the new arrivals was nineteen year old Latvian goalkeeper Elvijs Putnins, whose arrival I consider the main turning point in our season.

How did an obscure nineteen year old Latvian goalkeeper end up at Boreham Wood Football Club? Putnins was QPR's third choice goalkeeper and at the time they were flying high in the Championship under Neil Warnock and heading back to the Premier League for the first time in fifteen years. They had two very good goalkeepers already in Paddy Kenny and Radek Cerny and Putnins wasn't going to get a look in. As part of the sale of Simon Thomas to Neil Warnock's Crystal Palace in 2008, there was a pre-season friendly arranged before the 2009-2010 season between the clubs, and from my understanding, a lot of goodwill between Neil Warnock and our club. Being from a non-league background himself, Warnock was impressed with our academy and set up and what we achieved on limited resources. This goodwill led to the signing of Elvijs Putnins. The arrival of Putnins led to the long awaited departure of Ashlee Jones and added something we'd been missing since Tony Tucker left, a decent goalkeeper.

Other significant loan signings included Mike Cestor, the left back from Leyton Orient for the rest of the season (give or take a few trips back to The O's). He would prove a more than adequate replacement for Daniel Brathwaite would be missing for a few more weeks. Talented Woking forward Olu Sogbanmu also arrived on loan for the rest of the season to add some much needed height (and goals) alongside Ali Chabaan up front.

We Can Work It Out

Going into the Chelmsford City match on 15th January, Boreham Wood were on eleven points from nineteen matches, one point below Lewes and four points from safety. Despite our poor form, being four points from safety wasn't the end of the world and easy to claw back with a good run of form. However, Chelmsford City were in second place on goal difference behind local rivals Braintree Town. Our two league victories so far had been against Dartford and Weston Super Mare. Chelmsford would be a different proposition.

When I arrived at the ground that day I was greeted by someone at the club who said, "you should see this new goalkeeper". I assumed he meant the size of him. However, on seeing Elvijs Putnins' slight build I assumed he was referring to his quality. On entering the ground I noticed a very different atmosphere from the gloom of St Albans on New Year's Day, the negativity of Bishops Stortford or the embarrassment of Hertford Town four days earlier. Everyone seemed to be focused, from the manager to the players and even the supporters. All of a sudden the players had a new togetherness. The match was superb and the 2-0 win well deserved. Olu Sogbanmu gave us the lead in the seventeenth minute following a fantastic forty yard run by left back Mike Cestor. Jon Clements added the second goal in his last appearance for the club before returning to the States. Our defence of Moran, Wilkinson, Garrard and Cestor were on top form and we didn't look like letting anything in. Putnins didn't have loads to do but you can tell the defence was more comfortable with him behind them than the previous custodian.

Despite the win against Chelmsford, we were not out of the woods yet and went on to lose our next two matches. The big talking point at Havant & Waterlooville became national news. The incident was mentioned on the second to last page of The Sun and was the subject of many a radio phone in. With the score 1-0 to the home team on the eighty second minute, Ali Chaaban tried to give the ball back to Havant goalkeeper Aron Howe and ended up chipping him from forty yards and the ball nestled in the back of the net. He could have tried that a hundred times and it would never have come off. As per the rules, the goal stood. With the score 1-1 Boreham Wood had eight minutes to hold on for a much needed point. However, Ian Allinson instructed his team to let Havant and Waterlooville score what turned out to be the winner to address the injustice. I believe he was to receive an award for sportsmanship by the FA. Following the drama of this match we were at home to Welling United three days later. An early Greg Morgan chance should have given Boreham Wood the lead but a Welling goal just after half time sealed it for the visitors. We were now six points clear of safety and it looked like the Chelmsford win was just a false dawn. I was still confident as our performances had been good

After the Welling defeat, a vital 4-2 win at home to Maidenhead and a significant 1-0 win away at St Albans on 1st February (exactly a month after the hammering of New Year's Day) put us back on track. The St Albans game was particularly pleasing as they were a shadow of the team of New Year's Day, Effiong was average and we were very much in the ascendancy. At the time St Albans were facing an FA hearing for financial irregularities and would receive a ten point reduction helping consign them to relegation. On 1st February we were still four points behind them and second from bottom. A Greg Morgan goal just before half time was enough to seal it for us. This was my first trip to St Albans ground and I was far from impressed. I was shocked that such a nice area as St Albans had a football ground in such decay. The moss growing in the terrace looked a throwback to another century and the advertising hoardings had adverts for at least two companies that no longer existed (I used to do recruitment in the area). The following Saturday we drew 2-2 at bottom of the table Lewes where Luke Garrard picked up a worrying knee injury which fortunately wasn't as bad as it could have been but it kept him out for a few weeks. This was followed by a fantastic 1-0 win at second placed Farnborough with an Elliot Godfrey strike.

A 0-0 bore draw at home to Dorchester followed which was our sixth game unbeaten. The most exciting news that day was the return of Sam Hurrell from Woking on a permanent deal. His form at Woking had deserted him. Unfortunately he wasn't as good in his second spell with Boreham Wood either. The Dorchester match represented the last match for the club for Ali Chabaan who impressed since joining us a few months before. The club accepted a good offer from Chelmsford for his services. The evening of the Dorchester match, I took Mrs Lewis out for dinner to celebrate Valentine's Day (even though it was 12th February) simply because I went to Chelmsford City away on the Monday night. The Chelmsford match was another excellent performance and a Sogbanmu goal after half an hour gave us a well-deserved lead. However a clumsy late challenge on Greg Morgan by Chelmsford's Takumi Ake saw a yellow card when it should have been a straight red. Morgan, our best player up to that point played no further part. This was a major turning point and Chelmsford went on to win 3-1 in a bad tempered match which saw Assistant Manager Jason Goodliffe sent off following a heated verbal complaint about the injustice of the challenge on Morgan. He ended up standing behind the goal with us. Despite it being Valentine's Day, there was no love between the two clubs. Following the Chelmsford defeat, two new players arrived including forward David Bryant from Braintree as a replacement for Chabaan and future Glasgow Rangers and Swindon goalkeeper Wes Foderingham on a month loan from Crystal Palace as a replacement for Elvijs Putnins who was out injured for a few weeks.

After a 2-2 draw at home to Staines on the Saturday we won impressively at Thurrock on the Tuesday night (1st March). Amazingly this was our last midweek away league win for three years until we beat Maidenhead in 2014. We won one and drew two of our next three matches in March but lost away to Dover with a late Adam Birchill goal. Birchill scored forty one goals that season. On the following Tuesday, an impressive Farnborough turned us over 4-2 at home and a 2-0 reverse at home to Braintree followed. This was our fourth match without a win and left us just outside the drop zone. Fortunately three straight wins in April meant that we were safe. A great solo goal by Greg Morgan beat Havant & Waterlooville followed by a fantastic individual performance and hat trick by Mario Noto gave us a 4-1 win from 1-0 down away at Dartford. If you watch the match on YouTube (which I have several times) you can hear an excited voice shouting "it's in" when Noto takes a shot for his second goal. That voice is mine. As my voice would indicate, it was a goal from the moment it left his boot. Alongside Sam Hurrell's second goal against Dover, it was probably our best goal of the season. The Dartford match was my favourite game of the season and I'm sure the eight travelling Wood supporters out of a crowd of over a thousand enjoyed it. I took Sara and Harry to this game and I'd never seen Sara so enthusiastic at football. A 2-1 win at home to Eastleigh on Good Friday with two more Noto goals, mathematically confirmed our safety. By this time both my children had caught the bug and were attending matches. Both enjoyed the Dartford and Eastleigh games. And were more than happy to come to Basingstoke on Bank Holiday Monday. The 1-0 defeat at Basingstoke was disappointing as it looked like the players were already on their holidays. However the following Saturday, Boreham Wood rounded off the season with an emphatic 3-0 win at Meadow Park against already relegated Lewes with Risbridger, Wilkinson and Garrard all scoring their first league goals of the season. Just before the match, Geoff Wickens received his Supporter of the Year award for the 2010-2011 season on the pitch. (He wasn't attending the Presentation Evening). Geoff had been attending Boreham Wood matches since the early 1970s and deserved the award, especially as he'd moved to Reading from Boreham Wood some years earlier and still travelled to matches home and away. Unfortunately Geoff passed away in the summer of 2016 after a brave battle with cancer.

Having only lost four matches out of our final twenty, we avoided relegation with plenty to spare, finishing our first season in the Conference South in a credible thirteenth place. Following the Lewes match, it was once again time for the End of Season Presentation Night at the Holiday Inn. Without the wild celebrations of the event the previous season, it was a good opportunity to reflect on what turned out to be a very good first season in the Conference South. It was a great night for Mario Noto who won every award going in what was a fantastic season for him. I hope he has a big mantelpiece at home.

I remember having a long conversation with defender Ryan Moran that night. He hadn't quite matched the form of the previous season but alongside his teammates ended the campaign well. He kept apologizing for his poor form and I had to tell him it wasn't that bad!! I found him to be an extremely nice bloke and quite a character. I'm not sure he was quite as daft as his nickname "Trigger" would suggest. It did occur to me that his time at the club might be coming to an end. I was proved right as he left the club that summer for St Albans. His contribution to Boreham Wood Football Club was immense and his role to our promotion in 2009-10 will never be forgotten. His performance in the play-off final in 2010 might just be the best performance I've ever seen from a Boreham Wood player, especially given the occasion and the fact he scored the opening goal. Ryan Moran died of cancer in the summer of 2013 aged just thirty one having been ill for a long time. His loss was felt by everyone who knew him and those of us who watched him play.

Having ended the season well, all the signs were good for the 2011-2012 campaign. However, the second season in a new division is usually harder than the first as quite often, newly promoted teams become less of an unknown quantity. I was a bit concerned that some of our good players such as Putnins, Cestor, Wilkinson and Sogbanmu were only on loan and I didn't expect any of them to return the following season. It should have occurred to me that Chairman Danny Hunter and Manager Ian Allinson would have something up their sleeves regarding new signings!!

Spurs on the other hand finished the season in fifth place and amazingly got to the quarter final of the Champions League in their first ever season in the competition. At the time of writing, they are the last North London club ever to get that far in the competition.

2011-2012 SEASON

Changes

The summer of 2011 was a very interesting time for Boreham Wood FC. Mario Noto, Luke Garrard, David Bryant and Daniel Brathwaite stayed on from the previous season but it looked like the loan players Putnins, Cestor, Wilkinson and Sogbanmu would return to their parent clubs having had such an influence in keeping the club in the Conference South. The summer ended with a number of high profile signings and Boreham Wood FC suddenly became the talk of the division with people wondering how such a small club could sign such high calibre players.

The first of these new signings was a big centre half Charlie O'Loughlin who had played for Solihull Moors in Birmingham. Fortunately he relocated from the "second city" to Hertfordshire to train as an Architect at a local firm. He was to be an excellent player over the next three years and speaking to him, he reminded me of a nightclub doorman I used to know in Birmingham while at university (very friendly but I wouldn't want to get on the wrong side of him).

We signed three players who had been with Farnborough the previous season, goalkeeper Michael Jordan, centre half James Smith and midfielder Darryl McMahon. They had all been key to helping Farnborough to second in the Conference South behind Braintree the previous season before losing the Play off Final to Ebbsfleet United. From my understanding Farnborough had financial problems so a number of their squad weren't retained. Jordan was meant as a replacement for Elvjs Putnins and James Smith a replacement for Luke Wilkinson. As it happened both Putnins and Wilkinson returned to the club on the eve of the season on loan until January although Putnins stayed on and off for the rest of the season. The signing of Irishman Darryl McMahon was a particular statement of intent by the club. He has been in the "Conference South Team of the Year" in 2010-11 and was thought of as one of the best midfielders outside the Football League. McMahon also joined our PASE Academy in his first coaching role so became full time with the club. Other signings followed including former Charlton Athletic right back Osei Sankofa and Ali Chaaban, returning from Chelmsford. Another forward, Ollie Palmer arrived on loan from Woking until January and Inih Effiong returned after an impressive season at relegated St Albans. Darren Currie, former Ipswich and Wycombe midfielder joined from Dagenham & Redbridge. Currie also joined the PASE Academy and was appointed as Assistant Manager when Jason Goodliffe surprisingly left the club on the eve of the season.

Unfortunately Greg Morgan left the club after many years to join Chelmsford. Morgan was a local boy who had come through the ranks at the club. He was the first player that really impressed me when I started watching the team in 2008 but at the time Chelmsford was a bigger club and it was seen as a step up for him. Nicky Nicolau, Gareth Risbridger, Michael Kamara and Ryan Moran also moved on.

The newly shaped squad had a busy pre-season to look forward to. It appeared to be going well with a well-earned 2-2 draw with Watford, narrow defeats against Dagenham & Redbridge and QPR and wins against Hendon, Potters Bar and Billericay where an on fire Mario Noto scored from the half way line. It looked like Mario Noto was about to take his game to yet another level after an outstanding 2010–2011 season.

Wake Me up When September Ends

The annual Arsenal pre-season match occurred on a balmy Friday night in late July, when I decided to swallow my pride and attend. It was Sara's first ever night match and the first time I'd ever attended a match involving Arsenal that didn't involve Tottenham. When the man of the moment Mario Noto gave Boreham Wood an early lead, I probably celebrated more then I normally would. The joy didn't last long as Arsenal responding immediately and went in at half time 3-1 up. In the final twenty minutes the Arsenal youngsters ran rings around us especially when Ian Allinson brought on some of the young PASE players from the bench. Arsenal went on to score four more goals in a 7-1 rout. The last of those goals came with the final kick of the match. Unfortunately our talisman Mario Noto sustained a worrying ankle injury while trying to prevent the goal. After a long delay, Noto was stretchered off. I suspected straight away that it was serious. Noto had only missed two matches in the past two seasons both from suspensions. The original diagnosis of two weeks out was a relief but something in the back of my mind told me this was optimistic. The thrashing against Arsenal and the Noto injury appeared to end the pre-season optimism and it took the best part of two months to recover. The day after the Arsenal match I took Harry to watch a Boreham Wood X1 play at London Colney where we scraped a 2-1 win. This was followed up by a 2-2 draw at Hemel Hempstead and a defeat at Tooting and Mitcham.

The season started at home against Havant & Waterlooville and it couldn't have begun any worse. In the first couple of minutes. Havant scored the only goal of the match and

Luke Garrard sustained a nasty knee injury that sidelined him for three months. The following Tuesday we played Bromley away and once again I dragged my brother Elliot to the game. Luke Wilkinson who had been so impressive against Havant, joined Garrard and Noto on the injury list and we were lucky to only lose 4-0. Ali Chabaan didn't look the same player as in his first spell at the club and he left the club again soon afterwards.

The following Saturday we were away to the eventual champions Woking. With Noto and Wilkinson returning we played much better and gained a creditable 0-0 draw. At this time Pelly Ruddock our PASE graduate was getting more game time. This was the first match I brought Harry to where I didn't have to chase him around. He sat down for the entire match. Two days after the Woking match, I missed my first home game in 2 years (due to a prior arrangement I couldn't get out of) as we drew 1-1 with Basingstoke and David Bryant scoring the first of sixteen goals this season. I was missing again the following Saturday because of a stag do, as Boreham Wood beat Thurrock 2-1 to record our first win of the season. I did make an appearance at Staines Town two days later with young Harry where we lost 2-1. Young Simeon Akinola scored our consolation goal in injury time. The Staines match marked the debut for Mark Jones, our new left back signed following over five hundred games for Braintree. He shared the left back berth with Daniel Brathwaite for the rest of the season as ironically one of them seemed to always be injured when the other was fit. I didn't take to Mark Jones at first but he grew on me and was a very good servant for Boreham Wood for the next three seasons.

As September started, we made another trip to Weston Super-Mare but the only good thing about it was the massive portion of fish and chips I ate before the match! The

4-1 defeat was well deserved and a nightmare performance by centre half James Smith confirmed that he wasn't quite the player we thought he was. Smith left the club soon afterwards. Misfiring forward Ollie Palmer also left the club but did very well for the next two seasons at Havant & Waterlooville eventually making his way into league football. In actual fact Ollie Palmer is probably the most successful former Boreham Wood striker I have seen as he has since made over one hundred appearances in the Football League for both Mansfield Town and Leyton Orient. He certainly didn't look like a player of that quality at Boreham Wood. While at Weston, we found out that Mario Noto needed an operation on his ankle (I knew it was too good to be true) and would be out until January. As well as that, Darryl McMahon had ruptured tendons in his ankle and would be on the treatment table for three months. It was going from bad to worse with our three key midfield players out long term.

With this chronic injury list, we followed up the Weston defeat with another loss at home to recently promoted Truro City. Fortunately I missed my third home match in a row that day as we had a wedding at the beautiful setting of Greenwich Yacht Club. Our fourth league defeat in a row occurred the following Saturday away to Eastbourne Borough and again I was missing because of another wedding, this time my cousin's in Manchester. Due to a raft of social engagements this period was probably my longest barren run of games since the early part of the 2009-2010 season. I arrived back from Manchester that Monday in time for the home match against second placed Welling United. After four successive defeats we had to win. To fill part of the gap left by our injured midfield trio, Chez Isaac arrived on loan from Watford. Fortunately two Darren Currie penalties gave us a 2-1 victory in what was an impressive team performance against a good side. This was Currie's only significant performance in a Boreham Wood shirt. I remember that Welling match because a particular individual supporting the away team didn't like me very much and was constantly telling me to F-off for no apparent reason. It's just as well I'm not a violent man as I'd have been within my rights to lash out!!

The beginning of October saw the start of our FA Cup campaign in the Second Qualifying Round at Slough Town, a team two divisions below us. Again I was missing due to my debut appearance at the Oktoberfest in Munich to celebrate my brother's fortieth birthday. The team by all accounts played like they'd drunk as much as I had, having been unceremoniously dumped out of the cup at the first time of asking, losing 3-2 with former Wood striker Sean Sonnor scoring the winner.

The Kids Are Alright

After the weddings, stag do's and the Oktoberfest I was now officially skint but had more time to focus on watching my local team. The malaise that had been hanging over the club since the Arsenal pre-season game and the subsequent injury problems was lifting. We had stopped feeling sorry for ourselves and had come accept that our three key midfielders were injured long term. I believe there was a bit of a clear the air meeting between the players, manager and Chairman following the recent poor form. Darren Currie left the club and Darryl McMahon surprisingly replaced him as Assistant Manager. Despite his injury McMahon appeared to create quite an impression in the PASE scheme as a very good coach and a key character around the club, clearly destined for a very successful coaching career. I assume Darren Currie didn't create the same impression.

Prior to the Dartford match on 8th October we had fallen to third from bottom of the league having only won once in eleven matches. Michael Thalassitis arrived on loan from Stevenage to partner David Bryant up front. The Dartford match to some extend reminded me of the Chelmsford home game the previous season. It was the day the belief started to return. This "mish mash" of a team was starting to gel. The 3-1 victory was well deserved and started a fantastic run of seven wins in a row in all competitions with David Bryant hitting a rich vein of form, eventually winning the Conference South Player of the Month award for October. He scored the only goal in our next match at Hampton & Richmond in a game more memorable for one of the finest saves I've ever seen from Putnins in goal to deny future Wood player Charlie Moone. This game was a real back to the wall performance in a match we would have lost earlier in the season. Apart from thirty-three year old Mark Jones the rest of the team that day averaged twenty years old. David Bryant scored the only goal again the following Saturday at Dorchester.

In the build up to the Dorchester match Boreham Wood signed someone who was to become one of my favourite players during my time watching the club. Midfielder Sam Cox grew up playing in the same Spurs youth team as future England internationals Andros Townsend, Stephen Caulker, Ryan Mason and Harry Kane as well as Tom Carroll, Alex Prichard and Adam Smith. There hasn't been many better youngsters to have come through a Premier League Academy in recent years. The fact that Cox turned professional with some of these players was quite an impressive feat. In October 2011 Cox was in his second season at Barnet and wasn't in the team so a short term loan was agreed with Boreham Wood. This loan was eventually extended until the end of the season and bearing in mind his contract at Barnet was up in the summer, I was hopeful he would join us permanently. As well as being a very good hard working player, he came across as a nice bloke who always seems to have time for the supporters.

Two days after the Dorchester match we hosted Maidenhead United at Meadow Park. As I walked into the ground a very excited fellow Spurs supporter Derek Bumby (who worked on the tannoy) came up to me to tell me Glenn Hoddle was there. He was my childhood hero and I needed to go and say hello. However I didn't know what to say to him so initially bottled it. Fortunately I walked up to him with a more confident Mo who got him to autograph his programme. I nervously said hello and walked away. I failed to notice that former Wimbledon goalkeeping legend Dave Beasant was sat with him. Hoddle was watching because midfielder David Hutton was making his debut for Boreham Wood. Hutton a former Spurs colleague of Sam Cox was in the "Glenn Hoddle Academy". The match was dreadful but we held on to win 1-0, with Hutton scoring on his debut from the spot.

The following Saturday, Bryant scored again in a 2-1 win against Bromley and a hard fought win after extra time at Hertford Town in the Herts Senior Cup followed. Despite Luke Wilkinson being sent off early on, a brilliant Thalassitis hat trick was enough to beat Dover 4-2 the following Saturday to lift Boreham Wood up to eighth in the table. Appearing on the bench against Dover was another new signing Chet Johnson. He had impressed four days earlier playing for Hertford Town against us so the club signed him after the match. Johnson remained with us for three months but was used mostly as a substitute. Johnson's younger brother who would watch Boreham Wood when his brother was playing, went in to achieve short term fame as one of eight members of boy band "Stereo Kicks" who came fifth in the 2014 series of XFactor. and I had the fortune (misfortune) of seeing them live when I took my daughter Sara to the XFactor Live show at The O2 is early 2015. Please don't tell anyone.

What's Going On

With the form we were in, it was hard to believe that we wouldn't win again in the league until 21st January. The week after the Dover match, we lost our first league match for two months, 2-0 away at Welling United. Unfortunately I couldn't find my mate who was using the "industrial language" when we played them in September. We then draw 1-1 at Basingstoke before playing Dover again at home in the Third Qualifying round of the FA Trophy. Another goal by David Bryant settled the tie. Dover must have been sick of the sight of us.

On a cold Tuesday night at the start of December, we played Leverstock Green at home in the Second Round of the Herts Senior Cup. With Boreham Wood several divisions above our Herts neighbours, we expected to win comfortably. However even the return of Darryl McMahon from injury couldn't prevent a 1-0 defeat following a goal-keeping howler by Michael Jordan in the last few minutes. The following Saturday we hosted Cambridge United in the First Round of the FA Trophy. The match was switched to 1pm presumably to help stop any crowd trouble from the expected big crowd. However there was no big crowd and the attendance of four hundred for such a big cup game was incredibly disappointing. This wasn't helped by a number of supporters not being aware of the earlier kick off time. Once again, the local community failed to come out and support their club. The match was very close and we gave a good account of ourselves against Conference National opposition. However Cambridge scored the only goal of the match with fifteen minutes left and we ended up with nine men as Mark Jones and Justin Cochran were sent off. Two disappointing away defeats followed at Eastleigh and Chelmsford, neither match I attended. This led us to the Boxing Day clash where I took a newly potty trained Harry to his first match without wearing a nappy. We hosted Sutton United and took the lead early with a Thalassitis goal. I believe the match was devoid of entertainment (I don't know for sure as I was back and forward to the toilet with Harry) but it looked like our goal would be enough until a ninety fourth minute equalizer by Sutton made the final score 1-1. I missed the goal. You'll never guess where I was!!

Fortunately I avoided the return fixture on New Year's Day at Sutton United when, with the score at 1-1, the game was abandoned after thirty minutes following a biblical rain storm. Our match against Salisbury the following week was postponed as they were still in the FA Cup so come Farnborough away on 14th January, we hadn't completed a league fixture for three weeks. We travelled to Farnborough that day without any match practice and with as many as four players serving suspensions including Cox and McMahon. Michael Thalassitis returned to Stevenage following his loan spell. The depleted team lost 4-0 with all the goals coming in the first half. The following week, the returning Luke Garrard, playing his first football since the first minute of the season, helped Boreham Wood to an impressive 3-0 win against Weston Super Mare at Meadow Park. Billy Lobjoit who joined on a short term loan from Leyton Orient, scored two goals that day. We were mid-table in the league at this stage.

The Weston Super Mare match was the first time Garrard, Noto and McMahon played in the same team due to their injuries. However unbeknown to us it was to be the last time. A few days later Darryl McMahon left to join Eastleigh.

Apparently the south coast club had new owners and bags of money. They tried to sign McMahon before Christmas but the offer was rejected. They came back with a vastly improved offer in January and a very generous package for McMahon, both were too good to turn down. I wasn't as disappointed as some with this departure as although I rated him as a player, I felt Boreham Wood would have to build the team around McMahon and I didn't think this was feasible long term. Due to the stop start few months at Boreham Wood McMahon hadn't really got going so we weren't reliant on him. I was more concerned about missing him as Assistant Manager. It was a very good financial deal for the club and gave us the opportunity to reinvest in the squad. The equally impressive coach, Luke Garrard replaced McMahon as Assistant Manager. Around this time, Pelly Ruddock completed his move to Premier League West Ham United. This was another mark of the success of the PASE scheme. As far as I know, there was a reasonable transfer fee involved and a commitment for West Ham to play friendlies against Boreham Wood for the next two pre seasons bringing a full strength team. The expected big crowds for these games would bring much needed revenue to the club.

The following week we hosted leaders and eventual champions Woking with Charlie Hunter filling the gap left by McMahon in midfield. Despite Hunter's impressive performance, we lost narrowly 2-1 to a late winner. The match represented the last in a Boreham Wood shirt for Dagenham & Redbridge loanee Luke Wilkinson. He had performed brilliantly for over a year but it was time for him to go and make his mark in the Football League. Unfortunately within a few weeks he ended up at Conference South rivals Dartford where he won promotion to the Conference National via the Play Offs at the end of the season before returning to Dagenham. Things went well for him after that. He was Dagenham & Redbridge Player of the Year the following season before following their manager John Still to Luton Town where he continued to impress. It was great to see all his hard working paying off.

Following the Woking match, we had matches postponed against Salisbury and Tonbridge Angels and had to wait seventeen days until our next fixture on Valentine's Day, the rearranged match at Sutton United. I did the right thing by Mrs Lewis this year and didn't go, taking her out for dinner instead. We lost 2-1 but played very well apparently. The following fixture was at home to Eastbourne Borough which ended in a disappointing 1-1 draw. This match marked the debut for Boreham Wood for another loan player, Barnet winger, Mauro Vilhete. He appeared on the pitch as a late substitute and it became apparent quite early on that we were seeing something quite special. I can't remember a Boreham Wood player during the period covered by this book, who has made such a big impact in a short space of time and is technically the best player I saw at the club during this period. This period from mid-February to the beginning of April when Barnet recalled him was real value for money for Boreham Wood supporters.

Another significant signing appeared prior to the match at Maidenhead United the following week. Omar Riza had recently been released by Conference North side Histon and joined us for the rest of the season. Riza started his career in the same Arsenal youth team as Ashley Cole and he made one League Cup appearance from the bench for the Gunners in the late 1990's. Riza was now thirty two years old and would add some much needed experience to our front line. David Bryant had stopped scoring since Michael Thalassitis left and playing with someone of Riza's experience would only help him regain his goal scoring touch. The Maidenhead match was fairly even until David Bryant ended his goal drought after twenty seven minutes with a blatantly off side goal before a cracker from debutant Riza made it 2-0 at half time. Unfortunately I missed our third goal right at the end because I was taking a certain three year old to the toilet. It was scored by Osei Sankofa at the end of a sweeping move involving a number of players. I'm told it was our best goal of the season!! The 3-0 win was our first away league win since the end of October. Bryant scored again two days later to take the lead at Tonbridge but a late equalizer by the home team made the final score 1-1.

Early March saw the arrival of two players who would become legends of the club and play a significant part in elevating the team to a level many thought was unachievable over the next few years. Centre half Callum Reynolds joined the club, initially on loan from Tamworth, and wide player Graeme Montgomery joined on a permanent deal from Eastleigh.

Two goals each from Vilhete and Noto secured a 4-2 win at Havant & Waterlooville in early March. The following week we drew 2-2 at home to Dorchester. Charlie O'Loughlin was suspended that day and took his seat among us in the stand. I ended up talking to him for most of the game, mostly about Birmingham (where he was from and I used to live). Having not scored for the club yet, I suggested that when he does score he comes over to us to celebrate. I didn't expect him to carry this out. I didn't expect him to score!!

Go West

When the fixtures for the 2011-2012 season came out in July 2011, there was one match that a lot of Boreham Wood supporters had their eye on which was Truro City away. Under the Chairmanship of property developer Chairman Kevin Heaney, the Cornish club achieved four promotions in only six years, making their way up the football pyramid to the Conference South in 2011. I was hoping the match would be scheduled for August bank holiday when it was nice and warm. Cornwall was my favourite UK holiday destination and I imagined sitting on the beach in the morning and attending the match in the afternoon. However when the fixtures were released, the match was actually scheduled for Tuesday 13th March, a Tuesday night, bloody Tuesday!! My first thought was to give it a miss. However it soon occurred to me that with the fixture being in March, there was plenty of time to "find a way". I eventually agreed with Mo and Barry that we would go.

The six hundred mile round trip was by far the furthest distance I've ever travelled to a football match in this country so in order to break the journey up we decided to stay overnight. Mo was driving and I booked the accommodation. I called the Red Lion Hotel in a village just outside Truro only to be greeted with an "allo maate" on the other end of the phone. I did wonder at that point whether I'd called Cornwall or some East End pub until our genial host "Mick" explained that he was from Bermondsey and relocated to the West Country to run a pub. I booked the accommodation which was three rooms above the pub, perfect!

Paula thought I was potty going all that way for football and taking two days off work, as did my mother. I explained to them that "going all that way" was what made it worthwhile! The journey to Truro was fairly quick but we noticed fog appearing as we were passing Stonehenge. This fog was becoming heavier as the journey continued. At this point, we were starting to worry that the game may be called off. We arrived at The Red Lion Hotel at about 2pm. I demolished a burger and chips with apple pie and custard for pudding and we settled down into the pub for the afternoon. Despite still being full from lunch, I ate a Cornish pasty two hours later (You can't come to Cornwall without sampling one). Mick was quite a character and we exchanged a lot of banter over the course of the afternoon. He admitted he'd never heard of Borehamwood but was considering joining us for the match in the evening. I suppose being a Millwall fan, he probably wasn't used to watching decent football. As the afternoon turned into early evening, the pub started to fill up with a number of strange looking characters. We were observing conversations that were going on among them and couldn't understand a word that was being said. It was like something out of a sitcom. We managed to answer questions okay such as "where is Borehamwood?" or "who are Borehamwood? I thought I was being rude giving one word answers but had trouble understanding anything so had to be as vague as possible.

At about 6:30pm we left the Red Lion Hotel for the short car journey to Truro City's Treyew Road ground. "Millwall Mick" decided not to come as he had other plans for the evening. Two things came to my mind when we arrived at the ground, 1) The fog was really bad and I thought the chances of the match taking place was 50/50 at best. 2) If Truro City's ground was going to be the hub of sporting activity in Cornwall (these were the plans), then they'd need a lot more work done to the place. We went into the bar to discover that there were a few more Boreham Wood fans stupid enough to make this journey. Soon afterwards we left the bar to watch the players warm up. At that moment Luke Garrard walked out of the player's tunnel looking at us and laughing. In fact he was doubled up. He came up to us shaking each of our hands and said "You boys love it. You boys must love it". As he then walked onto the pitch, we could hear him giggling from twenty feet away!!

As for the team, Mario Noto had sustained a hamstring injury against Dorchester so missed out. It was the last we'd see of him in this injury hit season, a shame because Noto had returned to his best form in recent weeks. Young right back Lee Close made his debut at left back to cover for Daniel Brathwaite who couldn't get time off work. As we were wondering where to sit, we got collared by Truro Chairman Kevin Heaney who shouted "come and sit here lads". We took advantage of some Cornish hospitality and took our seats. I was praying that Baz would behave himself in front of the Truro Chairman. His occasional rants at opposition managers, players and referees are legendary at Boreham Wood! The match itself was a blur. We hardly saw a thing because of the fog and I fully expected the game to be abandoned. I couldn't see the other side of the pitch or either goal!! There is no doubt that had this been a local game it would have been abandoned. Truro took the lead after eleven minutes and David Bryant equalized a few minutes later. I would describe the goals but I didn't see either of them. In the second half the fog lifted but Truro scored the winner on the hour mark. It was a fairly drab encounter and Boreham Wood didn't really get going.

Following the match, the three of us returned to the Red Lion Hotel only to find it locked. I glanced through the window and saw Mick and another chap singing to some very loud music. Apparently the bar is quiet on a Tuesday evening so Mick uses it as an opportunity to "let his hair down" He eventually let us in and after a quick drink Baz and Mo retired to bed. Not wanting to miss out on an opportunity to have a few drinks, I remained in the bar. Mick let me choose some songs on his IPod so naturally some ska classics and songs by The Who and The Jam went on. Fortunately Mick knew the words to every song so we formed an unlikely singing duet. For the next few hours, it was like being at a Mod/Ska Music Festival! I was even allowed to top my pint glass up on several occasions. Mick and I ended up talking in detail about Millwall's football hooligan past. He went on to blame the rise of the Acid House movement in the late 1980s on the demise of football hooliganism in the UK. He rightly explained that "ecstasy" turned people from fighting each other to cuddling each other, as if it he was annoyed by it!! I could imagine Mick running around the football terraces in 1980's in a Union Jack t-shirt with "These Colours Don't Run" printed on the front. By 2:30 am after my eighth free pint I'd had enough and decided to go to bed as we were leaving early the next day. Baz had to get home for a funeral. The other chap in the bar with Mick never said a word all night!

The journey home was just as quick as the journey there. We got home by midday and after only four hours sleep the night before, I went to bed for a few hours before Paula and the kids got home.

Getting Better

Four days after Truro, Boreham Wood returned some of the way there to play at Salisbury City. It was quite rightly suggested by Paula that I sit this one out and I had no bargaining power left. We returned to winning ways by beating them 2-0 with goals from Vilhete and Riza despite losing Luke Garrard to a red card just before half time. Unfortunately left back Daniel Brathwaite sustained a broken ankle which kept him out for the rest of the season. After three years great service this was Brathwaite's last appearance for the club. Because of a previous postponement, we played Salisbury again, this time at home forty eight hours later. Despite a fantastic performance from Vilhete we only managed to draw 1-1 but I shouldn't be too hard on the players. The Truro and Salisbury trips over a period of a few days, must have taken it out of them.

It was around this time that most of our home matches started to be filmed. Up to then, we were often able to watch highlights of away games on YouTube but none at home. This changed in the 2011-12 season. By the mid to end of the season, almost all our matches being filmed by Ravit Anand from a company called "Football Exclusives" which started in 2011 to film and help promote non-league football. All of a sudden they'd have cameras at a number of non-league from Conference South downwards (The Conference National had their own TV deal). For some reason there seemed to be a fair bit of opposition to this broadcasting by clubs at our level and below, probably because various chairmen thought it would have an adverse effect on attendances. If people could watch the best bits in highlights format why attend the matches? This was an argument used by league clubs when Match of the Day started in the 1960s and when live league football started in the 1980s. It has been proven time and time again that TV coverage actually advertises the game and encourages people to attend. Why should coverage of non-league football be any different? I thought they did (and do) an excellent job promoting the non-league scene. Ravit would continue to film and edit our home matches until the end of the 2012-13 season when the club launched its own TV Channel. Since then, Football Exclusives have gone from strength to strength covering a number of games across the non-league scene.

The Saturday after the Salisbury game was one game I was delighted that Football Exclusives filmed. We went into battle against Darryl McMahon's expensively assembled Eastleigh side having been in great form following only one defeat in eight matches. What followed was probably the most complete performance I saw from a Boreham Wood team in the period covered by this book. We had six different goalscorers in an emphatic 6-1 win. The scorers were Reynolds, Bryant, Montgomery, Riza, Garrard and Cox. Amazingly there was no goal for man of the moment Vilhete. Charlie O'Loughlin's first goal for the club would have to wait. McMahon ironically scored for them. We were now on a roll with goals by Riza and Bryant securing a 2-0 victory at Dover Athletic the following week. This result was overshadowed by a worrying head injury to Sam Cox which left him spark out. Apparently when he came round he was talking nonsense so ended up in hospital despite wanting to go back on and play!! This was typical of Sam Cox, he'd have wanted to go on and play again even if he was not *compos mentis*. He would be out for a couple of weeks and would be wearing a head guard (similar to Petr Cech's) for the next two seasons.

Two days after the Dover match we were at home to relegation threatened Hampton & Richmond. We were decimated with injuries at this point and had an unfamiliar midfield pairing of Charlie Hunter and Callum Reynolds. We also lost Omar Riza to a hamstring injury just before half time. This match however will live long in the memory due to the performance of one man. Hampton were fighting for their lives and good value for their lead albeit from a dubious penalty after fifty one minutes. Just after the hour mark a great cross from Montgomery was met with a bullet header by 5ft 4in Mauro Vilhete out jumping two bigger defenders to make it 1-1. Was there anything this player wasn't capable of? He was good in the air too!! Suddenly it was all Boreham Wood and Vilhete nearly scored again before a David Hutton free kick came off the crossbar in the last minute. We thought that was it and we'd have to settle for a 1-1 draw. However Vilhete had the last word with a memorable individual goal in injury time to win it. It was harsh on Hampton but with a player like Vilhete in the form he was in, they could do nothing about it. The win elevated Boreham Wood to eighth in the league and the visitors were in deep trouble, eventually getting relegated.

After the match I was excited thinking about Vilhete's winning goal. If only we had got him two months earlier, we'd be talking play offs now. It reminded me of when I used to watch Paul Gascoigne at Spurs in the later 1980 / early 1990's. He'd score a great goal or play brilliantly and I'd be smiling about it for days. In the days after the Hampton game that smile suddenly disappeared with the announcement that Barnet recalled Vilhete, exercising a twenty four hour call back clause in the loan agreement. I'd assumed if the agreement was until the end of the season, that's when it would end. Although I was heartbroken, I couldn't blame Barnet for recalling him as they were in a relegation fight and it was obvious what Vilhete could bring to the table. With that in mind, I failed to understand why Vilhete was only given a total of ten minutes playing time for Barnet for the rest of the season!! What was the point in the recall? I was gutted when Barnet eventually stayed up. However because they'd stayed up, maybe there was a chance of getting him on loan again the following season.

To cover for the injury hit squad Boreham Wood recalled two strikers from loan spells, Simeon Akinola from Harrow Borough and Inih Effoing from Chesham for the last four games of the season. Four days after the Hampton match (on Good Friday) we were away at already relegated Thurrock and despite the injury problems we had enough chances to win easily. However a shock 1-0 defeat was our first league defeat since Truro in mid-February. We followed this up with a 2-1 defeat on Bank Holiday Monday at home to another relegation threatened team, Staines Town.

The following Saturday Sara and Harry both joined me as we hosted Farnborough at Meadow Park. We were eager to return to winning ways and avenge the 4-0 defeat against them in January. Cox and Riza returned from injury and our good form before the Thurrock match returned. Goals from Riza, Akinola and Effiong made it 3-0 before the moment we'd been waiting for. A Montgomery corner was met by a bullet header from Charlie O'Loughlin to score his first goal for the club and make it 4-0. O'Loughlin was as good as his word and as I came scampering down the steps from my seat, he ran towards me and when I went to hug him he responded. As the Boreham Wood FC website described "He ran straight to the band of faithful Wood fans who had been ordering a joint celebration from him should he score". They were right. The match ended 4-0 and I asked Ravit Anand from Football Exclusives if he could leave that celebration on when he was editing it and he duly obliged. Sara and Harry thought it was hilarious.

A week later O'Loughlin scored again, this time to secure a 2-2 draw at Dartford. This time there was no Brett Lewis for him to run to as I was back in Cornwall, this time on a stag do in Newquay. On the final day of the season we played Tonbridge Angels at home accompanied by a torrential downpour. Fair play to groundsman Daniel Hunter for making the pitch playable for the game to go ahead. Another entertaining match saw an excellent 4-2 victory to round off the season for Boreham Wood in eighth place with Mark Jones scoring his first for the club.

The awards night took place that evening, this time at the club rather than the Holiday Inn. During the evening the four different "Player of the Year" awards when to Sam Cox,

Charlie O'Loughlin, David Bryant and Osei Sankofa. It goes to show, this season was very much a team effort especially after things were looking so miserable early on. Mo and Baz jointly won the "Supporter of the Year" award having accompanied each other to plenty of away games. The excellent finish to the season and the fact we now had a settled squad, ensured we went into the summer of 2012 with plenty of confidence that we could compete for the play offs the following season.

2012-2013 SEASON

In the Summertime

While London was hosting the Summer Olympics, 2012 was another very interesting summer for Boreham Wood Football Club. More players from the previous season were retained than any other season since I started watching them. In the early part of the summer Noto, Garrard, Jones, O'Loughlin, Hutton, Reynolds, Montgomery, and Effiong committed for the 2012-2013 season. This was a sign of our growing togetherness and the belief that the club would now be competing for promotion rather than trying to avoid relegation. Mario Noto started to combine his playing duties with that of First Team Coach.

Elvjs Putnins left the club following the end of his loan spell. Having been released by QPR he was seeking a new opportunity higher up the football pyramid. Unfortunately this would be as good as it got for Putnins, He went onto to play for Woking, Harrow Borough and Maidenhead over the next few years which was a shame because he is a better goalkeeper than that. The other goalkeeper Michael Jordan also left the club having been a disappointment since arriving from Farnborough. Right back Osei Sankofa, left back Daniel Brathwaite and top scorer David Bryant also departed. PASE striker Simeon Akinola also left for regular first team football at Harrow Borough in the Ryman Premier League. This was a shame because I felt he was on the verge of breaking into the team. By 2014 he secured a move to Conference National side Braintree Town.

The Canvey Island goalkeeper James Russell arrived to replace Putnins and Jordan. Right back Sankofa was a hard act to follow but the inspired signing of Ben Nunn from Chelmsford more than made up for his departure. Nunn was the final piece of the jigsaw for the back 5 that would last the best part of two seasons (Russell in goal with Jones, Reynolds, O'Loughlin and Nunn). Former loanee Chez Isaac having been released from Watford joined us permanently. Forward Elliot Buchanan joined briefly but was to be the only summer signing who didn't perform. Donovan Simmonds joined from Dover only to leave again immediately for Chelmsford! A familiar face arrived from Chelmsford in return. Since leaving Boreham Wood the year before, Greg Morgan had suffered an injury hit season at Chelmsford and having been released, returned to Boreham Wood on the eve of the season. This was great news as I don't think he should have gone in the first place.

The questions on everyone's lips this summer centred on the future of two players whose futures were less clear cut. Omar Riza had done a great job since joining the club in February but there was always a thought that he was waiting for a bigger club. Having played at a higher level this was understandable. As the summer wore on this move to a bigger club didn't occur. Riza eventually did sign and the first we knew about it was when he was named in the starting line up in the first pre-season match against West Ham. This was a pleasant surprise. Midfielder Sam Cox had been released from Barnet and therefore a free agent. It was widely predicted that he would join Boreham Wood on a permanent basis and I know an offer was made to him. As far as I was concerned he was part of the club anyway so it was only a matter of time before he committed his future. Unfortunately as the summer wore on and we were well into our pre-season matches, Cox still hadn't signed. Perhaps he was waiting for another league club to snap him up. Unfortunately he ended up signing for Hayes and Yeading just before the start of the season. Hayes had just been relegated from the Conference National but had an exciting future ahead of them with a new stadium about to be built. Perhaps with this on the horizon, they were seen as a better prospect than Boreham Wood in the summer of 2012. Cox was given the captaincy at Hayes and Yeading and knowing him, he'd have enjoyed that responsibility. I still think back to that summer and think, what a difference it would have made had Cox signed for us. Perhaps we wouldn't have faded so badly by the end of the season.   We would however see plenty more of Sam Cox during the 2012-2013 season.

During the summer, plans were revealed for the new eight hundred and ninety seater West Stand at Boreham Wood Football Club The previous West Stand was constructed in the early 1970's and was not only clad in corrugated asbestos roof panels, but was in a very poor state of general repair. The new stand would give the ground a seating capacity of one thousand four hundred and twenty. Work would eventually begin on the structure in the summer of 2013 at a cost of just under £600,000. With these exciting developments off the pitch we now had a team who were capable of adding some exciting developments on it. It's fair to say that in the summer of 2012 there was great optimism at Boreham Wood Football Club.

That's Entertainment

This optimism was carried into our first pre-season match in July at home to a full strength West Ham United. The match was the first of two friendlies arranged as part of the Pelly

Ruddock transfer with the second one taking place the following pre-season. Boreham Wood secured an excellent 1-1 draw against the Premier League outfit with a second half goal by a resurgent Inih Effiong cancelling out Sam Baldock's first half effort. The match stuck in my mind because of a brilliant goalkeeping performance from James Russell. At last we looked like we had a quality permanent goalkeeper to replace Tony Tucker. We didn't know it at the time but for the next few seasons we didn't have to worry about needing a new goalkeeper.

Another Effiong goal secured another 1-1 draw, this time against Stevenage a few days later. Next up after Stevenage was Watford. The arrival of the Pozzo Family as new owners of the Championship club lifted the spirits at Watford after a few barren years but it was the appointment of former Chelsea legend Gianfranco Zola as Watford's new Manager a few days before the game that really captured the imagination. Fortunately for our club's bank balance the Boreham Wood match was his first game in charge. The crowd was vast and everyone wanted to shake hands and have photos taken with the little Italian. I got into the ground early and managed to speak to Zola briefly following his interview with Sky TV. He seemed a pleasant guy and from my understanding he was at the club quite late speaking to supporters. The match was another entertaining one with David Hutton scoring a cracker to equalize future Boreham Wood player Piero Mingoia's opener. A brilliant late penalty save by James Russell ensured another 1-1 draw.

A few days later the annual Arsenal pre-season match took place. Once again Boreham Wood went in front, this time through Omar Riza before three late goals secured a 3-1 win for the Gunners. An Arsenal youngster called Anthony Jeffery came on as a sub and tore us apart in the last few minutes. Three days later, a mixture of first teamers and some academy players played against Reading. This was the start of a tie up between both club's academies. An impressive performance by youngster Robert Hastings couldn't prevent a 2-1 defeat for Boreham Wood. This was followed by an away trip to Southern League Division One side Biggleswade Town and a comfortable 3-1 win against the manager's son and former Boreham Wood player Lee Allinson who had just joined the club. As the pre-season entered August we lost 3-2 in a gripping game against Barnet at Meadow Park and rounded off the pre-season with a 3-1 win at Arlesey Town.

Following one of the most enjoyable pre seasons in years, the team were confident going into the opening Conference South fixture at home against title favourites Eastleigh on 18th August. The match started with Mario Noto sustaining a hamstring injury after ten minutes but ended with an emphatic 3-0 victory inspired by an outstanding Inih Effiong who scored one and made two goals for Montgomery and Riza. At this stage my season was interrupted as I spent ten days on holiday in Israel to coincide with my cousin's wedding in Jerusalem. While I was away we drew against both Hornchurch and Chelmsford and won at Sam Cox's Hayes & Yeading. I only returned to the UK two days before the match at Truro City and unable to make a return trip to the West Country and therefore couldn't reacquaint myself with "Millwall Mick".

Before the Truro match Mauro Vilhete who had impressed so much while on loan from Barnet the previous season joined on loan again until January. This was fantastic news. Former Barnet forward Cliff Akurang also joined the club to add some much needed competition to Riza and Effiong up front.

The Truro match resulted in another defeat against the Cornish club. The most worrying thing about this match was the indiscipline from our players resulting in straight red cards for Ben Nunn, Charlie O'Loughlin and Luke Garrard who would all be suspended for three matches, at the same time. This was much more of a headache then the 2-0 defeat. Two days later we played Sutton United at home and I attended only my second match of the season. What followed was something quite sensational. Our 3-0 win didn't tell the whole story as this was possibly one of the most entertaining matches I've seen Boreham Wood play. It was end to end stuff throughout and Sutton were excellent despite the heavy defeat. Two unforgettable goals by Mauro Vilhete won the match for us. I was getting excited after this match as I felt Vilhete could almost win the title for us on his own. The goals he was capable of scoring would add a lot of points to our tally. He was that good.

This optimism regarding Vilhete didn't last though. Between the Sutton and Farnborough matches he returned to Barnet for some "light training" and ended up with a groin strain ruling him out for up to five weeks!! This was heartbreaking news for us. When Vilhete returned to the team a few weeks later, he wasn't quite the same player. Against Farnborough the following Saturday David Hutton replaced him and had a great game. Two goals by Riza and one by Montgomery ensured a comprehensive 3-1 win and Boreham Wood were in fourth place after seven games. A week later it was a trip to deepest darkest Kent to play Tonbridge Angels. Again my brother Elliot (who lives in Kent) joined us. This was the first of three matches that O'Loughlin, Garrard and Nunn were suspended. As well as that Vilhete and Noto were injured. Jerel Ifil joined as centre back and went straight into the team to partner Callum Reynolds. Due to the makeshift back line we were 2-0 down within seven minutes and looked like we were heading for a heavy defeat. However an excellent team performance from this makeshift side drew us level after sixty six minutes with goals from Riza and Hutton. At this point we were the only team who looked like winning. Unfortunately a minute later all our good work was undone when ace goal scorer Frannie Collins put Tonbridge back in front. Another goal in the last minute made it 4-2. I thought our performance for sixty minutes in that game was the best of the season given the circumstances and the players we had out. Unfortunately though, we had to wait a few more weeks to win a game from 2-0 down. I missed our next league game, a 0-0 draw at Bath City two weeks later due to another stag do.

It was around that time we lost Mo. (Don't worry, he's still with us). Mo has been a regular Boreham Wood supporter for over forty years and has always been a popular figure at the club among supporters and staff. He has always been the life and soul of the party and sitting and travelling to away games with him over the last few years was good fun. Unfortunately Mo and his family decided to sell their house in Borehamwood and move to Cambridgeshire. Although some of us have remained in touch with him since, his visits to Boreham Wood matches since have been minimal. When I think back to the glory of the 2014-15 season, I'm sad that Mo didn't share it with us.

Boreham Wood started October at home to Billericay on a Monday night and a brilliant Inih Effiong hat trick secured an emphatic 3-0 win. Unfortunately Luke Garrard who had just returned to the team following his three match ban sustained a nasty ankle injury that would rule him out for over three months. The next league match in mid-October was a hard fought 2-2 draw at Salisbury City with Akurang and Hutton on the scoresheet. After an excellent start to the season we were now in second place.

Promised You a Miracle

The FA Cup run of 2012-13 will live long in the memory. In four seasons of watching the team, it was the first decent cup run we'd had and well worth the wait.

There was no indication of what was to come when we were drawn away at Southern League side St Neots in the second qualifying round. Goals from Morgan and Riza were enough to seal a hard fought 2-1 victory despite James Russell being harshly sent off. (This was later rescinded). For the Third Qualifying Round we were drawn away again, this time at Spartan League team Northwood which was close to where I grew up in Pinner. This time an emphatic 4-0 win was enough to see us through to the Fourth Qualifying Round where we were drawn away at Hayes and Yeading.

I always find it annoying when we draw teams in our own division in cup competitions. I like the variety that these cup games bring and playing a team we beat only a few weeks ago is a bit of an anti-climax. Sam Cox's Hayes & Yeading side were on a good run of form and were just outside the play-off places. Due to Hayes's landlords Woking FC also being drawn at home in the cup, the match was played on the Sunday rather than the Saturday. By the time we arrived at the ground the draw for the First Round (proper) of the FA Cup had already been made. The winners would play at home against League One highflyers Brentford. This would have been a local derby for Hayes & Yeading so they were even more determined to win. What followed was something quite sensational!!

After fourteen seconds of the match, a mistake from left back Mark Jones led to a fantastic opener from Jerome

Anderson for the home side. Two minutes later an excellent curling free kick from Daniel Wishart made it 2-0, not the start we were hoping for. At this time I remember looking at my "slow" watch which still said 2:59pm! Baz said "I think we should go home". I assumed he was joking but I wasn't in the mood for humour. Sam Cox was bossing the midfield for Hayes and we weren't getting a look in. The tie definitely appeared over despite the fact we started to play reasonably well after about twenty minutes. After half an hour Harry decided he needed the toilet. While we were in there, my afternoon got worse (or so I thought). While Harry was doing what he was doing, a massive cheer went up from outside. I said something like "oh golly gosh Harry. It's 3-0" (using words not similar to that!). It was game over and another cup run looked like petering out. However I was pleasantly surprised when we got outside to find out it was 2-1, not 3-0!! That loud cheer had come from Boreham Wood supporters celebrating Mauro Vilhete's "consolation goal". The cheer was so loud I'd assumed it was from the home team.

By half time we were the better team and had been stringing passes together like we'd done all season so far. Cox's influence had waned and Chez Isaac was now controlling the midfield. Riza, returning from injury replaced Effiong at half time to add some much needed drive to our front line. After fifty five minutes with Boreham Wood very much on top, an excellent run by impressive Hayes forward Kudus Oyenuga took him into our penalty area where he went down due to a clear foul by Mark Jones. The referee Richard Kendall blew the whistle, penalty? No it wasn't. Instead of awarding a penalty the referee produced a second yellow card for Oyenuga (he'd been booked in the first half) and sent him off for diving. What should have been a penalty to them resulted in an unfair sending off instead. Oyenuga was livid; as were the Hayes players but the referee's decision had to stand. Not only were Boreham Wood in the ascendancy but we had a player advantage with thirty five minutes remaining. Despite this numerical advantage and the quality of football we were playing, we couldn't break down this resolute Hayes defence. However with only twelve minutes left on the clock the brilliant Ben Nunn struck a deflected shot that crept in past Hayes keeper Sam Beasant to make it 2-2!! . Two minutes later, Omar Riza latched on to Mauro Vilhete's pass to finish with aplomb to make it 3-2. The Boreham Wood supporters went beserk. Four year old Harry Lewis didn't really appreciate what's going on but enjoyed being thrown around nonetheless. I couldn't speak for the next two days.

The final ten minutes were fairly comfortable, especially as the home team were reduced to nine men when Tom Cadmore was also given his marching orders. The final whistle led to scenes of jubilation from Boreham Wood players and supporters. Sam Cox and his Hayes & Yeading side left the pitch extremely disappointed and hard done by. I was so excited; I didn't want to leave the ground. I didn't expect to be watching this type of match when I started supporting Boreham Wood in 2008. This was probably in the top five matches I've ever been too and at that stage it had eclipsed the 2010 Play-Off Final as the happiest I'd been watching a Boreham Wood match.

The Brentford tie in the First Round was only thirteen days after the Hayes & Yeading game. Boreham Wood had been without a sponsor so far that season following the end of the agreement with Cardif Pinnacle. In between ties a new sponsorship agreement was confirmed with Barnet & Southgate College (the club's PASE Academy partners) which would bring some much needed revenue into the club. The match itself was overlooked for live TV but did appear as the main match on the ITV highlights show. For the first time since I've supported Boreham Wood, I had to buy a ticket in advance with a seat number on it. Part of the build up to the game also centred on Charlie O'Loughlin. O'Loughlin was facing suspension for the Brentford game and his appearance in the big cup tie was somehow dependant on the Wingate & Finchley v Hitchin FA Trophy match the week before. If the FA Trophy fixture didn't result in a replay, Boreham Wood would play Hitchin Town the following Tuesday in the Herts Senior Cup and O'Loughlin would therefore be suspended for that game rather than the Brentford FA Cup match. If the FA Trophy match was a draw, the replay would take place that midweek instead of the Herts Senior Cup game meaning O'Loughlin would miss out on the Brentford match. (Confused?). To cut an even longer story short, a late Hitchin equaliser secured a 2-2 draw and a replay. O'Loughlin did miss the Brentford game. This gave young Ben Jefford an opportunity to play at centre half alongside Callum Reynolds. Jefford was in the Reading Academy and joined Boreham Wood on loan to gain some regular football. Despite his impressive performances when called upon, he hardly played due to the outstanding form of our other defenders. I was pleased for Jefford that he got the chance against Brentford and he certainly didn't let us down.

When the day of the match arrived, a decent crowd of fifteen hundred turned up. Earlier chances for Hutton, Akurang and Montgomery should have put Boreham Wood in front but we were undone by an excellent individual goal by Brentford's Clayton Donaldson after sixteen minutes. The rest of the first half developed into a ding dong encounter with Boreham Wood still having the best of it with Riza hitting the crossbar after a great team move. Harry Forester gave Brentford a 2-0 lead just before half time, effectively ending the match as a contest. By half time we were definitely the better team but were 2-0 down. I felt that if we could get one back early in the second half we had a chance, but we were not playing Hayes & Yeading here. Brentford were at the top end of League One so were more than capable of seeing this game out. The visitors failed to add to their lead in the second half mainly due to an outstanding performance by James Russell in goal. However Boreham Wood couldn't get going after the break and the match ended in what was eventually a well-deserved 2-0 win for Brentford.

While our great FA Cup adventure was over for another season we had gained a lot of positives from it. The extra revenue for the club was important. The Hayes and Yeading match will live long in the memory. Unfortunately, following our cup exit, our performances in the league never really recaptured the early season form.

Sara and Harry are up for Cup. Prior to the Brentford match in 2012

Too Much Pressure

Coming back to the league, Boreham Wood were away at Weston Super Mare the Saturday between the two cup ties. I didn't go and when I found out we were 2-0 down I was pleased I didn't make the trip. However for the second week running, we came back from two down to win, this time 4-2 with an unbelievable goal by Greg Morgan the main talking point.

Unfortunately the hangover from the Brentford defeat lasted for the next few weeks. Two days after the FA Cup defeat we were away at Hitchin for the rearranged Herts Senior Cup tie. Fortunately I missed the 3-0 defeat as Sara wanted me to take her to a fireworks display in Meadow Park. I hate fireworks with a passion and find these events boring and a waste of money. However I'm pleased I went there instead of the Hitchin match. The following Saturday we were away at Histon in the FA Trophy. Histon, a village team, enjoyed a great recent history spending time at the top end of the Conference National and knocking the mighty Leeds United out of the FA Cup live on TV. However Histon were now on the slide. They were at the lower end of the Conference North and the good times were coming to an end. Despite Histon's situation, they were by far the better team that day and we were fortunate to still be drawing 1-1 heading towards full time. I was pleased to be taking them back to Meadow Park for a replay. Unfortunately for Histon their PA announcer put her foot in it by announcing the price of the supporters coach for the replay. Inevitably, Boreham Wood grabbed a late and undeserved winner through Graeme Montgomery to make it 2-1.

Two days later we were back in league action hosting Basingstoke at home. We were now fourth in the table but with games in hand due to our cup exploits. Unfortunately a rare goalkeeping error by James Russell gave Basingstoke the lead early on and a Riza penalty late on salvaged a 1-1 draw. This was followed by a well-deserved 1-0 win at Dover Athletic with Ben Jefford scoring the winner. The following Saturday we were back in FA Trophy action at Bromley. I missed the tie because I was in Blackpool on a lads weekend with my brothers and some of their friends to coincide with the Watford game up there. While Watford squandered a 2-0 lead to draw 2-2, Boreham Wood were dominating Bromley only to be hit with a late Bromley equaliser to secure a 1-1 draw and a replay two days later. A severely hungover Brett Lewis made it back in time for the replay fully expecting a home win but Bromley were good value for their 2-0 win and our cup adventures were over for another season.

The following Saturday, (1st December) we were at home to Weston Super Mare. Apart from the Brentford cup match this was our first Saturday home match since 8th September. (That's twelve out of thirteen matches away from Meadow Park) a heroic effort by players and supporters. We went into the Weston match having only lost twice in the league, with our last defeat on 15th September and were also unbeaten at home. With that in mind, we expected a clear victory against a poor Weston Super Mare team. However, we stumbled to a disappointing 1-0 defeat on what was probably the coldest day I have ever had watching Boreham Wood. Young Harry was so cold he spent most of the second half in the club shop by the heater where he actually fell asleep. Clearly the match wasn't anything to write hope about. A week later we were at home again, this time to Truro City. Truro were a shadow of the team we played the season before. Their Chairman Kevin Heaney who was so hospitable towards us when we went down there, had been declared bankrupt and ended his financial support to the club. The club was on the brink of being thrown out of the league until two local businessmen put up the money for them to finish the season. They were in administration and rooted to the bottom of the table. They could only field one substitute against Boreham Wood. Despite that, they worked their socks off to secure a 0-0 draw and could have won it had James Russell not saved a penalty. A week later, we returned to winning ways with a 3-0 victory at play off rivals Farnborough with goals from Riza, Morgan and Nunn. This match marked the debut for centre forward Luke Norris who we signed on loan from Brentford. After good starts to the season Effiong and Akurang had been disappointing so we needed another forward to partner Riza.

The Hayes & Yeading home match on 22nd December was postponed just before kick-off due to a massive downpour making the pitch unplayable. This led us into the Christmas period where a late Ben Nunn equaliser secured a deserved 1-1 draw at Staines on Boxing Day. Three days later we were away at another play off rival Chelmsford, a match that we dominated missing a hat full of chances until Riza scored the opener just before the hour mark. Unfortunately a brilliant equalizer from frequent Boreham Wood nemesis Anthony Cook made it 1-1 before Kyle Vassell scored the winner for the home team. This was hard to take as we should have won by some distance. On New Year's Day 2013 Boreham Wood repeated their 1-1 draw with Staines, this time at home with Norris scoring his first for the club. Over the next week we beat both Eastbourne Borough and Maidenhead 2-1 at home before an enforced three week break occurred due to snow and ice.

During that period, matches against Salisbury, Eastleigh, Welling and Havant & Waterlooville were postponed and there were a number of changes in personnel at the club. Omar Riza was surprisingly released with David Hutton.

Vilhete returned to Barnet following the end of his loan spell. His form had dipped over the last couple of months but he finally broke into the Barnet team on his return. Luke Norris returned to Brentford following the end of his short loan spell. Three new forwards arrived including Michael Thalassitis, returning from Stevenage on loan, Lewis Toomey from St Albans and Loick Pires from Woking. Wide man Piero Mingoia arrived from Watford as a replacement for Vilhete. On paper they looked like good signings but unfortunately only Thalassitis really contributed.

On 28th January we played at home to Hayes & Yeading in a rearranged match following the postponement in December. For most of that day, it looked like going the same way. I arrived at the ground at 7pm and it had been raining "cats and dogs" since about midday. I was waiting for the inevitable postponement but amazingly it didn't happen. The rain soon stopped and the pitch was holding up well. Again credit to Daniel Hunter the groundsman. The Boreham Wood performance that night mirrored some of those shown early in the season. Goals by Thalassitis, Noto and Montgomery secured a deserved 3-0 win. In the last few minutes Hayes forward Kudus Oyenuga got his second harsh red card of the season against Boreham Wood following a heavy challenge on Ben Nunn. The incident was right in front of us and it should have been a booking at best. Oyenuga was absolutely raging and as he walked done the tunnel and was shouting "fcuking Boreham Wood. Always fcuking Boreham Wood". It's amazing to think that twelve months later he joined us!! It was good to see Luke Garrard return after four months out to take his place on the bench. Despite Sam Cox's endeavours Hayes and Yeading were not as good as they'd been earlier in the season and were beginning to slide down the table. Their Manager Nas Bashir lost his job two days later. Off the pitch they were in financial trouble and the building of their long awaited new stadium was put on hold as they finished the season flirting with relegation. The form of Sam Cox led to him winning all their Player of the Year Awards, a great achievement, but it was an indication that he was carrying a poor team.

February started with an away match at eventual champions Welling United on a Tuesday night. Fortunately I didn't attend and for almost the first time this season we were totally outplayed going down 4-0 against a very good side. Apparently it would have been more but for James Russell in goal. Our first Saturday match in five weeks produced a stale 0-0 draw at home to Bath City. A week later we played Bromley away and were hanging onto fifth place (the last play-off spot). I managed to rope both my brothers into coming to the game. We dominated for the most part, even after Mario Noto was sent off just before the hour mark. Montgomery scored a fantastic header soon afterward but Bromley equalised with five minutes to go. With the score 1-1 Lewis Toomey ran half the length of the pitch in the last minute but with the keeper to beat somehow missed the target. I was gutted following this result because it seemed like a defeat. I suspected that day that despite Boreham Wood being in a play-off spot all season, we weren't going to make it. The players were running out of steam. These fears were put to bed for a short while, four days later when an excellent encounter at home to Salisbury produced a 1-0 win with Chez Isaac scoring the winner, his first of the season. An entertaining but feisty 1-1 draw at home against Dover followed with a lot of bickering among supporters and players. For some reason Dover fans and players didn't like Charlie O'Loughlin!! He would wind them up. Dover player Ian Simpemba was sent off late on after elbowing him. I missed the next game away at

Maidenhead. However due to heavy traffic the players nearly missed it too!! They arrived just before kick-off. It's probably no surprise that we were 2-0 down in the first 20 minutes until a late Thalassitis goal made it 2-1. Boreham Wood was still hanging on in fifth place.

We started March with a well-deserved 4-2 win against Tonbridge Angels with Pires scoring twice. Amazingly this was the third 4-2 scoreline in a row between the clubs. A week later I took Harry on the train to watch us play at Dorchester. Our normal travelling companions Baz and Linda didn't go so I thought we'd do something different. Unfortunately despite the three hundred chances we seemed to create, the match somehow ended 0-0 despite a Dorchester player getting sent off for trying to cripple Greg Morgan just after half time. This incident caused a massive row between me and a Dorchester fan who accused Morgan of diving. In fact I felt like I was arguing with the whole stand. My language at this point can only be described as industrial. A few days later, we secured a very good 1-1 draw away at Eastleigh due to a late O'Loughlin header. The following match was away at relegation threatened Billericay Town. Two new signings were involved that night including wide man Jerome Anderson from Hayes & Yeading and free scoring forward Charlie Moone from Hampton & Richmond. This match followed the usual pattern with Boreham Wood dominating but only managing a 1-1 draw. We won the following match 2-1 at home to Hornchurch on Good Friday and maintained our position in the play-off places. This wouldn't last though.

Burnout

Following the Hornchurch victory we only won one of our last eight matches and eventually finished well outside the play off places. It wasn't helped by the fact we had to play eight matches in April, however due to the poor winter weather the same thing would have applied to most clubs. I missed the 2-1 defeat at Sutton on Bank Holiday Monday but understand that it was again a good performance where we didn't take our chances. The following Saturday we recorded only our second home league defeat of the season, losing 2-1 to Dorchester with the away side scoring a late winner. It was our first back to back league defeats of the season and the play offs were becoming a distant dream. Another 2-1 defeat three days later at home to Havant & Waterlooville almost sealed our fate. We would be playing Conference South football again in the 2013-14 season. In mid-April we travelled to Basingstoke in treacherous conditions. It had been raining all day and I'm amazed the game went ahead. We recorded our first win since Good Friday when two Thalassitis goals secured an impressive 3-2 victory.

Following the Basingstoke match we drew the next two matches 1-1, away to Eastbourne Borough and at home to Welling United. The result in the Welling match all but confirmed the visitors as Conference South Champions. They had a big turnout that day and it was great to see their players and supporters celebrate together. I felt a tinge of jealousy because for a long time it looked like we'd have something to celebrate. The following Tuesday we played our penultimate game of the season at home to Bromley. Again Boreham Wood took the lead with Charlie Moone netting on seventy two minutes. However two goals in the last few minutes sandwiched by a Montgomery penalty miss, turned the match on its head with Bromley winning 2-1 with the last kick of the game. At this point I couldn't wait for the season to be over. We had one more match, away at Havant & Waterlooville on the final day of the season. This game followed the pattern of recent matches. We were playing well but losing. The match, like the season was petering out until a moment of magic at the end made us all feel slightly better. Youngster Robert Hastings came on as substitute with two minutes to go and in virtually the last kick of the match hit a fantastic dipping shot from the edge of the area to make it 1-1. This was in my opinion the best goal we scored all season and confirmed the promise that Robert Hastings was beginning to show. Hastings went off to celebrate with Chairman Danny Hunter who just happened to be standing behind the goal. The Chairman was obviously delighted that his PASE scheme had produced a player who could score a goal like that. I think the general consensus after that goal was that Hastings would feature prominently for the club the following season. Unfortunately this didn't happen and that stunning last minute equalizer at Havant was as good as it got for him. Hastings only played occasionally the following season before being loaned out to Harrow Borough. I'm not actually sure what happened to him after that. It's a shame because he had so much talent.

Following the match, I bombed it back to Boreham Wood in just over an hour to get ready for the Presentation Evening. This year it was slightly different because it was the club's sixty fifth anniversary and the event returned to The Holiday Inn in the larger of the two function rooms. A number of former players and personalities from the past were among over two hundred guests. This year the four players of the year awards were split between Callum Reynolds, Chez Isaac, Charlie O'Loughlin and Ben Nunn. Like other Presentation Nights, this was an extremely enjoyable occasion that followed a pattern from previous years as I managed to eat at least two dinners (without spilling anything down my white shirt). Apart from the Chairman and the Manager, Mark Hughes and I were the last to leave at 2:30am.

The 2012-13 season ended up being an anti-climax as Boreham Wood finished up ninth in the table, some ten points off the play off places having occupied the top five for most of the season. The football we played up to our cup exit against Brentford was definitely the best I'd seen at Boreham Wood apart from the 2014-15 season. However we got progressively worse as the season went on. Some of our signings in the New Year weren't up to it and players who'd impressed early on looked jaded. Unlike the previous three seasons, we didn't finish on a high. Having said that we got to the first round of the FA Cup for the first time in nine years and ninth place would have been an achievement in the past. Our expectations were increasing year on year.

The players went on another post season break to Puerto Banus and I finished the season accompanying my friend Gavin to Grosvenor Vale to watch Wealdstone in the Ryman League Play Off Semi Final against a team called Concord Rangers. Wealdstone were clear favourites against the Essex upstarts and dominated the match from start to finish. By the eighty ninth minute, Wealdstone only had a 1-0 lead to show for all their chances. Inevitably Concord equalized with the last kick of the match and went on to score the winner in extra time. While Wealdstone had to wait another year for promotion to the Conference South, Concord went up by winning the Play Off Final at Lowestoft. I didn't know it then but Danny Cowley's Concord Rangers side were to prove a thorn in the side of Boreham Wood over the next couple of seasons. They were a team with a low budget who didn't seem to know when they were beaten.

Goodbye Cruel World

A couple of weeks after the 2012-2013 season ended, I along with a few other Boreham Wood supporters, attended a charity match at Chesham United football club. It was a "Ryan Moran Select XI" v Chesham United. We found out some months earlier that former Boreham Wood player Ryan Moran had been suffering from cancer and this match brought together a number of players who Moran had played with throughout his career to raise money for various cancer charities. I took Sara to the match and it was an enjoyable occasion. Ryan Moran and his parents were delighted to see some Boreham Wood supporters there and Ryan his usual friendly self, despite being desperately ill.

Sadly Ryan Moran passed away a few weeks later at the age of thirty one. I found out about his death on Twitter via a tweet from former Boreham Wood player Lee Allinson and news of his passing spread like wildfire throughout the football community. Suddenly there were a host of tributes from people in the game including one or two Premier League players. Although I didn't know him that well personally, I was extremely upset to hear the news. A memorial charity match was arranged a few days later on the pitch outside Birchfield Leisure Centre in Hatfield (Moran's home town). This time it was Ryan's Postie's XI against an Arsenal celebrity XI. A lot of people turned up on a very hot day to pay tribute. I went with Harry, Linda and Barry and we had an enjoyable time and it was good to see a number of players and supporters there from all the clubs that Moran had played for. As Boreham Wood's pre-season fixtures started, there was one minute applause for Moran before the matches against West Ham and Luton Town.

The contribution Ryan Moran made to Boreham Wood football club during his two spells at the club was immense. He was a big part of the team that got to the semi-final of the FA Trophy in 2006 and having left the club soon afterwards, he returned in 2009 and played a key role in helping the club to promotion to the Conference South including a man of the match performance (and the opening goal) in the 2010 play-off final win against Kingstonian. More importantly he seemed a thoroughly decent chap and it was hard not to feel for his wife, parents and sister. He will never be forgotten by Boreham Wood supporters who were fortunate enough to watch him play.

Ryan "Trigger" Moran who did so much for Boreham Wood FC. RIP

With Mario Noto and the FA Cup in 2013

2013-2014 SEASON

Summertime Blues

After a disappointing end to the 2012-13 season it was obvious where our problems lay. The backbone of the team was still very good but we desperately needed someone to put the ball in the back of the net. Russell, Nunn, Jones, Reynolds, O'Loughlin, Noto, Garrard, Morgan and Montgomery committed for the 2013-2014 season. However, Michael Thalassitis who had performed well since returning on loan in January, returned to Stevenage and was eventually sent out on loan to Conference South rivals Ebbsfleet United for the 2013-14 season. Thalassitis had a moderate season at Ebbsfleet and unfortunately tore his anterior cruciate ligament in the last minute of their Play Off Final against Dover which kept him out of the game for a year. Charlie Moone returned to Hampton & Richmond where he once again proved to be a prolific goalscorer, Lewis Toomey joined Hemel Hempstead in the Southern League and Cliff Akurang left for Bishops Stortford. This meant we started the 2013-14 season with none of the forwards from the previous campaign. Unfortunately Chez Isaac also left for pastures new, joining Conference National side Braintree Town.

During the pre-season we signed forwards Donovan Simmonds and Callum Willock following their release from Dover. I was particularly pleased with the signing of Willock because I remembered him excelling against us at Ebbsfleet in 2010 when we lost to them twice in a week. Perhaps he would be the answer up front. Another former Ebbsfleet player, Ricky Shakes arrived from Kidderminster. This was an impressive signing as he'd been part of the Kidderminster squad that had just been pipped for the Conference National title by Mansfield Town. Shakes could play either in midfield or on the right wing. Midfielder Mark Bentley joined from Hayes and Yeading but left for Wealdstone in the first few months of the season when he lost his place in the team. Another Hayes & Yeading player, Sam Cox announced he wouldn't sign a new contract there because he was looking for a way back into full time football. Fellow Hayes & Yeading players Calum Butcher and Kudus Oyenuga signed for Scottish Premier League side Dundee United and it looked at one stage like Cox was also heading to Scotland to join Morton.

The summer of 2013 also brought some positive news away from matters relating to the first team. Construction of the new West Stand would start in mid-July following the Arsenal pre-season match and Boreham Wood FC's own Television Channel "Boreham Wood TV" was launched to cover all the home matches. For a number of years Arsenal Ladies, the best women's football team in the country, played at Meadow Park. Prior to the 2013-2014 season it was agreed that the men would get in on the act with the "Arsenal Development squads" including their Under 19 and Under 21 teams also playing home games at Meadow Park. The Under 19's team included a Champions League competition whose group stage would mirror that of the "real" Champions League. This was great coup for the club. The town would have the opportunity to watch all these matches free of charge. While I don't like Arsenal, I appreciate the linkup between the clubs and the commercial benefits it brings to Boreham Wood FC. These commercial benefits have often been overstated though. If I got a pound for everyone who thinks our success is due to a massive financial gift from Arsenal Football Club, I'd be a rich man. Sometimes I get annoyed that so many non Boreham Wood fans seem to have seen our accounts when I haven't!

Our first pre-season match was against Premier League West Ham at home. This was the second of two pre-season matches confirmed as part of the Pelly Ruddock transfer in 2012. Before the match, there was a generous one minute's applause for recently departed Ryan Moran nicely observed by both sets of supporters. Unfortunately that's where West Ham's charity ended as they finished up convincing 3-0 winners. If it hadn't been for James Russell in goal, it would have been more.

One name was missing from our team sheet for the West Ham match and other subsequent pre-season games. New signing Ricky Shakes was nowhere to be seen. I wrongly assumed he'd left the club already without playing a game, just like Simmonds did the year before. I couldn't have been more wrong. It soon emerged that shortly after signing for the club he sustained an extremely nasty Achilles tendon injury in training that would keep him out of action for at least six months. This was heartbreaking for the lad and disappointing for the club who had a well paid player under contract missing for most of the season. There was also a worry as to what sort of player Shakes would be when he returned. This type of injury has ended careers or at least reduced the effectiveness of a player. Was Ricky Shakes going to be this all action hard working player we signed? The answer to that question was emphatic to say the least. However we weren't to know that in the summer of 2013. During his period of enforced absence, Shakes joined the PASE scheme as a coach. It was useful that he was around the club to feel part of things. He was also on hand for many sessions that the club physiotherapists put him through. With a lot of hard work by all concerned, he returned to first team action in March 2014 with twelve matches of the season left.

Next up after West Ham, was Conference National side Luton Town. Luton under recently appointed John Still, were finally about to embark on a season that would end their five year absence from the Football League. Boreham Wood beat them 1-0 with a goal from Simmonds. The following week was the annual match against an Arsenal X1. Usually the team Arsenal put out would include a few fringe first team squad players and a few youngsters. For some reason this year it was just an Arsenal youth team. This annoyed a lot of local Arsenal fans I know who at least expected to watch some players they'd heard of. Despite their youth, we knew the Arsenal team would be hard working, fit and would play some nice football. However the older Boreham Wood team walked all over them that day. Goals from Montgomery, Noto and Willock led to a convincing 3-0 win. The Arsenal side that day included Anthony Jeffrey and Austin Lipman.

The follow Wednesday we hosted Brentford at Meadow Park. A friendship and mutual respect had developed between the clubs since the FA Cup match the previous season and this was the first of what became an annual pre-season fixture. Brentford had heartbreakingly missed out on promotion to the Championship in the Play-Off Final at Wembley. However like Luton Town, they would put that right by winning the League One Title convincingly in the 2013-14 season. An impressive performance by the visitors resulted in a 3-1 victory. Next up were another losing play off finalist Watford. The "Golden Boys" had had a great season the year before, playing some fantastic football and got very close to automatic promotion before losing in the play-off final to Crystal Palace. Gianfranco Zola's side wiped the floor with us winning 6-1. Boreham Wood wrapped up the pre-season by losing at home to Cambridge and beating Potters Bar Town away 4-0. Unfortunately Callum Reynolds was injured in the Potters Bar match and missed the first two months of the season. Just before the start of the season, wide man Matty Whichelow arrived from Watford on a permanent basis and midfielder Matt Ball signed from Stevenage on loan until January.

Time for Action

The season started on 17th August away at Tonbridge Angels with the new players Whichelow and Ball going straight into the squad. Charlie O'Loughlin was the new team captain and two excellent goals from Matt Ball secured a convincing 2-0 win. A few days later we drew 2-2 at home to Bishops Stortford in a match we probably should have lost. Another fantastic goal from Matt Ball was the highlight of the night.

The day after the Stortford match it was announced that Sam Cox had rejoined the club for the 2013-14 season. This was a real surprise because I was under the impression he'd joined Morton in Scotland. However for some reason it didn't happen. Their loss was our gain. We knew what we were getting with Sam Cox and he would add something to our team. Cox would once again go on to prove his worth. Despite Cox not having a pre-season, he made his debut against former club Hayes & Yeading the following Saturday. This was not the Hayes & Yeading of a year ago though. Like us, they had a poor second half of the previous season and began to slide down the table. In the close season they lost their three best players Cox, Calum Butcher and Kudus Oyenuga and appeared to be in some financial trouble. The building of their new ground had been put on hold and they were in an expensive groundshare arrangement with Woking. Despite

Hayes's woes, Sam Cox arrival and Boreham Wood taking an early lead, Hayes and Yeading ran out deserved 3-1 winners. It didn't help that we were now missing O'Loughlin for a couple of weeks out injured.

Two days after the Hayes defeat we were back in action away at Staines Town. Unfortunately our injury problems at the back got worse when Ben Nunn and Luke Garrard came off injured, both would be missing for a few weeks. Once again, we lost 3-1. Fortunately O'Loughlin returned for the following match at home to Eastleigh who were flying high. Unfortunately Mark Jones chose a very inconvenient time to get married and go on his honeymoon. He would miss almost all of September. By the time "he and Mrs Jones" came back from their trip we "had a thing going on" where we were virtually propping up the table!! You can't blame Mark Jones, bearing in mind his break would have been agreed before he signed his new contract in the summer and a fully fit squad would have been able to absorb his absence for a few weeks. We were well beaten 3-0 by the eventual league champions Eastleigh. We followed that up a week later with another 3-0 defeat this time at Weston Super Mare which was the first game I'd missed this season. After four defeats in a row we were staring down the barrel somewhat with injuries and poor form from those who did make it on the pitch. Following the Weston match, Calum Willock left the club. He'd been a disappointment and seemed half the player who'd been so effective playing against us for Ebbsfleet years earlier. Having lost four on the bounce, the next match against newly promoted Gosport Borough was crucial. Alex Pike's Gosport team hadn't won a game and were finding life in the Conference South very hard since promotion. Our 2-0 victory, although unconvincing, was most welcome. Eventually Gosport managed to adapt to life at this level combining an excellent run to the FA Trophy final at Wembley with a great run at the end of the season to finish twelfth despite an incredible fixture pile up.

A few days after the Gosport win, we returned to losing ways with a 2-0 reverse at Farnborough. The following Saturday I dragged my long suffering brother Elliot and his son Finn to Ebbsfleet United away. He continued his record of not seeing us win since Dartford away in 2010 but this time he had to stand through a fairly drab 0-0 draw with the home team denied a blatant late penalty. The Ebbsfleet line up included former Boreham Wood players Michael Thalassitis, Osei Sankofa and Darryl McMahon. McMahon had recently joined from Dover for a fee of £13,000 and was now playing for his third club since leaving Boreham Wood less than two years earlier. Following the Ebbsfleet game, Boreham Wood acquired some much needed firepower with the arrival of Billy Lobjoit, now on a permanent basis from Leyton Orient. However it was another forward, PASE graduate Raheem Sterling-Parker who came up with a well-deserved ninety third minute equalizer in the league at home to Bromley at the beginning of October. I missed this match as I was once again at the Oktoberfest in Munich for another delightful weekend of drinking beer and eating meat. Our next league match resulted in a 1-0 defeat at Basingstoke.

Around this time, new loan signing David Moli arrived from Wolverhampton Wanderers to add some more firepower to our strike force. Moli had been a bit of a child protégé moving from the Luton Town academy to Liverpool's one when he was younger as if he was supposed to be the next big thing. Somehow he ended up at Wolves and then Boreham Wood on loan in what would be the first of two spells with us. Despite the fanfare, Moli was a disappointment and quite why we ended up signing him again a year later on a permanent basis, is beyond me. Moli's two spells at Boreham Wood conjured only two goals.

Our next league match at the start of November was away at Chelmsford City. This was the debut for another loan signing, Arsenal forward Austin Lipman. I was undecided as to whether I should go as I had my fortieth birthday party at the football club that night. I was tempted to go as all the preparation could be completed before leaving for the "Melbourne Stadium". However Paula persuaded me not to. Our league form had been awful with only two wins in eleven league games and we were now in the bottom three. I also wasn't a fan of going to Chelmsford FC as the athletics track around the ground made it a poor view and we always seemed to lose there. However this wasn't the same Chelmsford side we'd played previously who had always seemed to be there or thereabouts as far as the play offs were concerned. The ridiculous decision for them to sack long serving manager Glenn Pennyfather and replace him with the untried Dean Holdsworth following the play off semi-final defeat at the end of the 2012-13 season, was coming back to haunt them. Like Boreham Wood they were now struggling at the wrong end of the table. What followed that afternoon made me reluctant to ever miss a game again! We ran out 6-0 winners following an excellent performance with two goals from Montgomery and goals from Lipman, Moli, Matt Ball and Robert Hastings. Apparently it should have been many more. Some Chelmsford supporters even clapped us off at the end. Dean Holdsworth was rewarded with his P45 and Boreham Wood gained a morale boosting victory at the start of a very important month.

Orange Juice Blues (Blues for Breakfast)

The FA Cup run of the 2013-14 season was almost as thrilling as that of the previous season. It nearly ended with the clubs first ever victory over a league club but finished in gut wrenching heartbreak and a scandal over a jug of orange juice!

The cup run almost never got off the ground. We were drawn away at Barton Rovers in the Second Qualifying Round. Ian Allinson's former side were in the Southern League Division One which was two divisions below us. We were extremely lucky to get away with a 0-0 draw at Sharpenhoe Road in the first match as the home team were the better side. Fortunately we completed the job two days later in the replay with a comprehensive 3-0 win with goals from Cox, Noto and Simmonds.

We followed that up with a tough away match in the Third Qualifying Round at Maidstone United. Maidstone had just been promoted to the Ryman Premier Division and had free scoring former Tonbridge Angels player Frannie Collins in their ranks. They had a massive support base having recently returned to play in the area following a few year's ground sharing with Ashford Town. Maidstone's new Gallagher Stadium was a lovely state of the art ground with an artificial pitch. I would have made the home team favourites and if you'd offered me a replay I'd have taken it. However Callum Reynolds return to the starting line-up for the first time this season helped us considerably. An own goal and a Luke Garrard penalty ensured a comfortable 2-0 victory. The result was tainted to some extent by a stupid sending off. Donovan Simmonds had lashed out after being tackled and made a lonely walk down the tunnel. This was his last appearance for Boreham Wood and the first I knew of his departure was hearing that he'd signed for Tilbury! Despite a lot of promise,

Simmonds had been a disappointment and his discipline left a lot to be desired. Maidstone's infrastructure helped ensure promotion again, this time to the Conference South (or the renamed National League South) at the end of the 2014-15 season. I think they will be heading back to the Conference National or even back to the Football League in the not too distant future.

To non-league supporters the draw for the Fourth Qualifying Round of the FA Cup is always exciting. It is one step away from a potential tie with one of the big boys in the third or fourth tier of English football. The draw took place two days after the Maidstone match and was live on Talksport radio station at 10:30am. I took a break from work to listen to the draw and was delighted to hear we would play Ryman League North side, Heybridge Swifts at home. Although we couldn't underestimate them, we had to be happy with that. In a tightly fought match against a well organised Heybridge team, Matt Ball scored the winner with seven minutes remaining and we were in the First Round of the FA Cup for the second season running. Following the Heybridge match I appeared on "The Non-League show" on Radio Five being asked about Boreham Wood's cup run.

The following day I followed the cup draw on Twitter while eating a large steak at the "Miller & Carter" steak restaurant in Stanmore. Our nice cosy family Sunday lunch was interrupted by the news of another home draw, this time against League One side, Carlisle United. I was happy with this as they weren't as good a side as Brentford the year before and thankfully it was at home so I fancied our chances.

Over nine hundred supporters packed into our three sided ground (construction of the West Stand was well under way) for the Carlisle match which was memorable for an excellent Graeme Montgomery turn and shot that was brilliantly tipped over by Carlisle goalkeeper Mark Gillespie. If Monty's shot had found the net, it would have been good enough to replace Ronnie Radford's famous goal for Hereford against Newcastle at the beginning of the TV highlights show!!

The match ended 0-0 and there was stark realization that we were going all the way to Carlisle ten days later for the replay. Although the journey was an identical distance to Truro the year before, we had less preparation time. I'd already provisionally booked the Tuesday off work but didn't have the annual leave left to take off the Wednesday as well. The initial news from the club was that there wouldn't be any transport for supporters. My usual travelling buddies Barry and Linda wouldn't be coming because Baz had just had a knee replacement operation and the journey was too far for Linda. The train wasn't an option as we wouldn't be able to get back that night. Within a couple of days I had the journey all planned. I found a National Express coach that would leave Golders Green on the Tuesday morning to arrive in Carlisle at 4pm. The return journey would leave Carlisle at midnight arriving at Victoria at 5:30am following a full night's sleep on the coach (hopefully). I would have a shower and change of clothes at Victoria station and head straight to work. Paula thought I was mad. Having made this decision I was quite excited about the journey. For whatever reason I delayed booking the coach by a couple of days and in that time the club announced that they would be laying on a coach for supporters after all. This would leave the club at 11am, returning straight after the match which suited me.

On the day of the trip to Carlisle, I woke up early as I did a Bootcamp fitness class at 6:15am, on the Astroturf at Boreham Wood Football Club. Before that I went for a 5k run. Believe it or not I was starting to get quite fit at the end of

2013. I started the Bootcamp in January 2013 and managed to keep it up three times a week. In the summer I'd also taken up running for the first time in my life. By 7am my exercise routine was over and after a much needed shower I had the rare treat of dropping the kids to school. I then had the first of two radio interviews on BBC Radio London who were reporting on the match that night. Before meeting the coach at the club I completely ruined my fitness regime by going to the Toby Carvery for an "eat as much as you like breakfast". It wasn't healthy but set me up nicely for the day.

The coach journey was very pleasant with plenty of banter and a few beers being drunk. Fortunately the coach boasted a toilet. The journey had been fairly quick so with time to spare, it was decided we would stop off at a pub in Penrith just south of Carlisle for a couple of hours. We found a very pleasant establishment near where the coach dropped us off and proceeded to have a few drinks followed by a trip to the local chippy. By the time we got to Carlisle's Brunton Park ground at 7pm I was quite drunk. On entering the stadium I remembered I had another interview with BBC Radio London at 7:15pm. This was going to be live on air just before their live coverage of the England v Germany international match at Wembley. Gone was the muttering stuttering interviewee from this morning to be replaced by a more confident performer due to the volume of alcohol consumed. The interview lasted about five minutes and was mainly to do with Boreham Wood's chances which I thought were very good.

Before the match we managed to lose one of our supporters while entering the ground!! I'd never met Sean Browne before this night but on the way up to Carlisle I found him to be a pleasant chap, good company and he has since become quite a good friend. Sean had successfully travelled on the coach to and from Penrith without any hitch but disappeared once we entered the ground!! No one had his phone number and the "Wood Army Facebook group" was still over a year from being founded. Sean failed to make it to the match and also didn't make the coach home either. Apparently he got disorientated while trying to get in the ground and informed he wasn't welcome. He then spent the rest of the night walking around Carlisle (probably swearing at himself) before he managed to find a hotel desperate enough to take him in before embarking on a very expensive train trip home to London in the morning. There is a rumour, it may have been the booze!! I have "dined out" on this story many times over the last couple of years. Sean Browne – if you are reading this, you are a legend!!

By the time the match started the "Wood Army" were in fine voice. The team responded with an excellent display. Montgomery shot just wide early on with the keeper well beaten. After twenty eight minutes former Spurs player and French international Pascal Chimbonda brought down Austin Lipman in the penalty area and Luke Garrard stepped up to bury the resulting penalty for a well-deserved 1-0 lead. Garrard came over to celebrate with the supporters. It was a great moment. Two minutes later we were in dreamland. It was David Moli's turn to get fouled in the box and Luke Garrard had the opportunity to make it 2-0 from the spot. Unfortunately a fine save from Carlisle keeper Greg Fleming kept the score at 1-0. Surely there would have been no way back for the home team if this had gone in. The match continued with Carlisle having most of the possession but not looking like scoring. Unfortunately with eight minutes left on the clock, Carlisle forward Lee Miller equalized with a header from a cross to make it 1-1. This was a body blow considering we seemed to be holding on comfortably. A few minutes later the fourth official signalled five minutes of injury time. With seven seconds of that remaining, Carlisle substitute Mark Beck scored the winner to break our hearts. This was an awful experience especially as we'd played so well and were more than capable of beating a poor Carlisle team. After the match we just wanted to get on the coach and go home. I slept for almost the whole journey and we arrived back at the football club at 4am. I grabbed two hours sleep in my own bed before getting up for work.

What followed with the players after the match wasn't known to us until the following day. Apparently when Carlisle scored their winner they were goading some of the Boreham Wood players, a poor show from a team seventy four places above Boreham Wood in the football pyramid. It was reported by someone from Carlisle United that Boreham Wood players had urinated on the floor in the dressing room and damaged the changing room door and placed the teapot in the urinals. The truth was that left back Mark Jones clearly riled by the outcome of the match and the treatment by Carlisle players at the end kicked out at a plastic jug of orange juice sending the contents across the changing room floor. The changing rooms were disgusting and apparently wouldn't have looked out of place at County League level. The door was already damaged with lots of different holes in it anyway. Apparently the teapot had been perched on a small table and was put in the sink by one of our club's staff so it would fall off. To add to the injustice, the Boreham Wood players were not fed and there was a distinct lack of hospitality from the home club. The squad had to rely on a plate of sandwiches ordered at their hotel. This was a disgrace and has left a lot of Boreham Wood supporters and staff quite bitter towards Carlisle United Football club. Their subsequent relegation from League One that season was very pleasing. It's just a shame they couldn't follow it with back to back relegations the following season (although they came close) which would have led to us playing them in the league. That would have been karma. Let's just say, we weren't about to arrange any pre-season friendlies against Carlisle United!!

After the War

A few days before "Orange Juice Gate" we were at home to Gloucester City in the Third Qualifying Round of the FA Trophy. We lost 1-0 to a poor Gloucester team due to an error by skipper Charlie O'Loughlin continuing our poor run in the competition since reaching the semi-final in 2006. The hangover from the Carlisle defeat continued the following Saturday due to a 1-0 defeat at Eastbourne Borough which put Boreham Wood in the bottom three. The following Tuesday we started impressively at home to Maidenhead United going 2-0 up in the first ten minutes, only to end up drawing 2-2. This was followed by a home defeat against Bath City. Fortunately we saw the back of David Moli at the same time. In early December we played Bath City again, this time away from home and a stoppage time equalizer by PASE graduate Karl Brown secured a point in a 2-2 draw. .

At this time we signed forward Anthony Jeffrey on loan from Arsenal to add some much needed pace to our attack. Jeffrey's contribution over the next three months was immense and he carried our forward line for that period helping us turn our season around. Two days later we were excellent against Sutton but somehow managed to lose 3-1 despite Montgomery scoring from a shot similar to that against Carlisle in the home match. This time it went in. The following Saturday we played Weston Super Mare at home. This match was memorable to me because of the poor crowd. Only 115 people bothered to turn up and I put a very irate message on

Facebook moaning about the lack of support. We drew 1-1 taking us out of the relegation zone on goal difference.

The arrangement with Arsenal's Under 21's team led to a very bizarre night on 20th December when I did something I've never done before and am never likely to do again. I was at home flicking through the channels on Sky and came across Man United TV which was showing live coverage of their Under 21's match at Meadow Park against Arsenal. I decided to watch the first half of what was a very enjoyable match while letting the world and his brother on Facebook know that Boreham Wood's Meadow Park was on live TV!! At half time I left the comfort of my armchair and drove to Meadow Park to watch the second half at the ground. I'm definitely the only person I know to have watched the first half of a match on TV and the second half at the ground!! Ironically I spent most of the second half talking to someone and hardly watched a thing.

Rumble in Brighton

It sounded more like a science fiction character rather than a semi pro football team. However this weird team called Whitehawk in the east of Brighton, having been promoted three times in four seasons, now had a football team in the Conference South. Being very fond of Brighton and watching Boreham Wood away, there was no doubt I was going to this game especially as it was a six pointer between two sides at the lower end of the table. The fact that it was on 21st December, the Saturday before Christmas, was the icing on the cake. I'd rather stick pins in my eyes than go shopping with the missus or anyone else's missus for that matter, especially three days before Christmas. I have been to Brighton many times as a kid and more recently as a father taking my kids. The previous summer the kids and I had a great time there on a very hot day. With this in mind young Harry couldn't wait for the Whitehawk game and another trip to his favourite seaside town. (I can't wait until he's old enough to watch Quadrophenia)

It was clear that when the four of us (me, Baz, Harry and his Spiderman umbrella) arrived at Elstree & Borehamwood Station that today would be very different. It was cold, raining and windy and even though we doubted that the game would be on, we set off for Brighton anyway, via a brief change at Farringdon. It all started to go a bit wrong when we changed at Farringdon and realized Harry left his Spiderman umbrella on the previous train. Never mind, "The rain is bound to ease off. He won't need it anyway". I then had a look at Twitter and there was every indication that the game will be called off. I then "checked in" on Facebook as I passed East Croydon to be bombarded with messages such as "you're mad". I received a very reassuring message from Grant Morris from the club that the game is likely to be called off. We continued on our journey though as even if there was no game I was determined to complete the Harry Ramsden's Challenge!!

On arriving at Brighton Station it became clear that the weather was actually worse than when we left Borehamwood. In fact the gentle sea breeze was actually a force ten gale! Despite Baz recently having a knee replacement he was happy to walk to Harry Ramsdens as I'd assured him it would only take about ten minutes. The subsequent forty minute walk was harrowing. I was trying to prevent a five year old boy from being swept into the road while attempting to stay on my feet in probably the worst wind and rain storm I've ever witnessed. If Harry hadn't foolishly left his Spiderman umbrella on the train it surely would have collapsed under the pressure. Normally a similar walk along Brighton seafront would result in me subconsciously re-enacting and quoting the scene from Quadrophenia where they are chanting "We are the Mod" with fists clenched in the air. I always resisted the temptation to throw a chair through the window though!! This walk was unfortunately quite different and was all about staying on my feet and protecting my five year old son who I dragged to this windswept location to watch a game that had almost no chance of taking place!! We eventually reached Harry Ramsdens soaking wet but Baz and I completed the Harry Ramsdens challenge with the minimum of fuss in the set timeframe and were to be proud recipients of our free t-shirts and certificates!! Young Harry found it amusing, the amount of food we ate and that he was in a location he thought was named after himself!!

At this point having looked online it appeared the match might actually take place because it hadn't been called off even though it was already 2pm and every other senior match taking place in Sussex had fallen foul of the weather!! A cab was ordered to "The Enclosed Ground" Whitehawk. The cab ride was amusing as we eventually got to a country lane, then another country lane and then what seemed like about four more country lanes until we got to the ground. 2:15pm at this point and the match had still not been called off.

As we entered the ground, the horizontal rain and wind was a sight for sore eyes. It was like a scene from "The Omen". I half expected a spear to fall from the church straight into me!! The players were only just arriving having been in horrendous traffic and their frivolous demeanour gave me the impression that they thought the match wouldn't happen and were merely "going through the motions". Their apparent sing song on the minibus on the way while stuck in a massive traffic jam on the M23 perhaps backed this up!! It seems, the match WAS called off, however the referee who made that decision "wasn't at the right level" and when the "real" referee turned up he confirmed the match would go ahead.

It became obvious that we were never going to break any crowd records for away support that day as most people had taken the sensible decision not to travel all the way to Brighton for a match that had little or no chance of taking place. In fact the official crowd of fifty six (surely the lowest ever in the sixth tier of English football) must have been overestimated because Harry only counted a maximum of twenty five people despite having four attempts at it. As well as that, the Whitehawk ground is probably the sort of place where you can go in through gaps in the fence and therefore your attendance wouldn't show up on any official attendance figures. The so called "party army" of Whitehawk supporters must have been doing their Christmas shopping that day.

The match itself was dreadful and had 0-0 written all over it until a brace of goals from Anthony Jeffery gave us a 2-0 win. Apart from the players sliding around, the match was memorable for the constant singing of "Wood Army" between us and the group of four blokes behind the goal (who happened to be Sam Cox's dad Terry and some of his mates in Brighton on a jolly up). This was only our fourth league win of the season and our first since the incredible 6-0 victory at Chelmsford some seven weeks before.

Apart from the vastly expensive cab ride to the station, the journey home was fairly straight forward and uneventful apart from Harry singing "Wood Army" at me at every opportunity, expecting a response!! We never did find his Spiderman umbrella but the Harry Ramsdens certificate had pride of place on my mantelpiece and the t-shirt is still in my wardrobe waiting for me to lose enough weight so I can fit into it.

Let's See Action

After our amusing trip to East Brighton we would play newly promoted Concord Rangers on Boxing Day. Since watching Danny Cowley's Concord side overcome Wealdstone in the Ryman League Play off Semi Final the previous season, they had struggled in their first season at this level. This was another massive game. Fortunately I missed the match as we had plans I couldn't get out of. We were comprehensively outplayed and lost 2-0. This Concord side eventually managed to finish an incredible ninth place, a testament to their hard working team ethic and Danny Cowley as a manager. It became apparent that he was destined for better things.

Two days later we went to Bishop's Stortford in what was an incredible match full of incident and some controversy both on and off the pitch. Concord Manager Danny Cowley sat in the seat behind us to run the rule over the Boreham Wood side who they were due to play again on New Year's Day. As you can imagine, plenty of banter was flying around. Baz being Baz apparently fired plenty of stick at him on Boxing Day, had to take a more measured approach now!! I reminded Cowley how lucky his Concord side was against Wealdstone the previous season which he agreed with. During the match Boreham Wood played some of their best football of the season particularly in the first half when we should have had more than the 2-0 lead given to us by Jeffrey and Noto. Early in the second half, Bishop's Stortford scored from a penalty to make it 2-1 and what followed can only be described as a melee between most of the players on the pitch. For some reason Greg Morgan and Stortford scorer Reece Prestedge were singled out for straight red cards. The whole of the Bishop's Stortford management team including manager Rod Stringer were then sent to the stand. After this Boreham Wood were hanging on quite comfortably. In the last few minutes the brilliant Anthony Jeffery was brought down in the area and Noto converted from the spot again to ensure a 3-1 win. Unfortunately Mark Jones then went on to earn a stupid red card by attempting to push a Stortford player into the dugout!! Wood boss Ian Allinson immediately and wisely signaled for Jones to head straight to the changing rooms to avoid any post-match incidents. At the final whistle Baz had an altercation with a twelve year old boy who for some reason kept staring at him and eventually knocked his hat off his head and threw it onto the pitch. Mario Noto kindly gave it back to Baz but at this stage all the Stortford crowd could see was Barry having a go at a child!! I can honestly say that Barry did nothing wrong. I can only assume that they don't teach their children manners in this part of Hertfordshire. I understand what it may have looked like to the watching Bishop's Stortford supporters though. We were threatened with violence and I even had an off duty policeman threatening to arrest us!! I was trying to imagine Harry being thrown into the back of a police van with handcuffs on. Surely he'd have been the youngest supporter ever to be nicked at a football match! However "PC Plod" accepted my explanation of "Barrygate" and kindly let us go. The Stortford match and the excellent form of Anthony Jeffery was a big turning point of our season. We now had a team that was playing together. Maverick individuals like Donovan Simmonds and David Moli had gone and we now had a squad full of players we could depend on with Anthony Jeffery adding the much needed quality up front. However, our disciplinary record left a lot to be desired at times. Although Greg Morgan's actions were out of character, we still had players like Charlie O'Loughlin and Mark Jones who despite their qualities, were sometimes like a time bomb waiting to go off. Due to the forthcoming bad weather Greg Morgan's subsequent three match ban lasted until 1st March!

For the next couple of months our fixtures were decimated by postponements due to severe flooding. We had only four matches in the whole of January and February. Two weeks after the Stortford game we were back in action at home against fellow strugglers Dorchester United. This was a very one sided affair with Boreham Wood running out 5-0 winners. We didn't have a match for the next two weeks and in that time Anthony Jeffrey left the club as Arsenal had terminated his contract and he joined Wycombe Wanderers with immediate effect. Austin Lipman returned to Arsenal soon afterwards leaving us very short upfront. In response to these exits, Ian Allinson signed two forwards on loan from Wycombe Wanderers, Junior Morias and Lee Angol. At the time I wasn't very excited as losing Jeffery was a major blow to our season. If I had the choice between keeping Jeffery or signing Morias and Angol I'd have kept Jeffrey, especially as the last forward we signed on loan from a league club was David Moli. That's why I'm not a football manager!! Neither of our two new strikers had convincing records. Morias, eighteen years old, came through the ranks at Wycombe and had failed to really impress despite making a number of appearances for the first team, albeit a lot of which came from the bench. A short term loan at Ryman League Hendon earlier in the season wasn't particularly successful either. Nineteen year old Lee Angol had come through the ranks at Spurs and joined Morias at Wycombe. He'd played even less for the Buckinghamshire club than Morias and was perhaps regarded as not as good as him. Angol also played on loan at Hendon and failed to really shine there either. Despite these misgivings, what followed was an absolute tidal wave and proof that Ian Allinson had the ability to see something in a player that others couldn't see. It was a masterstroke that Boreham Wood are still benefiting from now and it has given a lot of people including myself a lot of pleasure. From my understanding when Allinson went to watch Morias play, he was also struck by this other raw centre forward (Angol) and ended up signing him as well. I could be wrong but signing the second forward may not have been part of the initial plan. Surely this was the best double signing since Spurs bought Ardiles and Villa from Argentina following the 1978 World Cup.

Boreham Wood returned to action on 25th January at home against Dover Athletic. Morias was in the starting line up with Lee Angol coming on as a late substitute. An entertaining encounter ended in a 2-2 draw. Before the next game against Basingstoke at home, we added another loan striker to our ranks. Kudus Oyenuga, formerly of Hayes & Yeading had joined Dundee United in Scotland during the summer but was struggling to break into the team. Oyenuga had a history with Boreham Wood having been unfairly sent off in his last two matches against us. I can imagine his opinion of Boreham Wood hadn't been that high. However he had impressed at Hayes the season before so I felt would be a good addition to our ranks. Although I rated Oyenuga, he was overshadowed by Morias and Angol during his short time at the club and was often used as a sub. He would eventually return to Dundee United the following season only to be loaned out to Cowdenbeath for the whole season. In the summer of 2015 he left Dundee United for Hartlepool United in League Two. His stock had suddenly risen when it emerged he had been the strike partner of Harry Kane in the Spurs youth team. Kane had come from nowhere to be a real force during the 2014-15 season for Tottenham.

Oynenuga made his debut against Basingstoke alongside Junior Morias upfront in an entertaining 1-1 draw with Morias looking particularly impressive. After this match we were left with another frustrating nineteen day gap until the next game which would create a massive fixture pile up where Boreham Wood would have to play eleven matches in March and nine in April. We returned to normality on 22nd February at the home of league leaders Bromley. We were 2-0 down early on but dominated the match following the sending off of Bromley's Rob Swaine after twenty five minutes. A Luke Garrard goal gave us hope but a string of missed chances kept the score 2-1 to the home side.

It was hard to believe that by the time of the Tonbridge Angels home match on 1st March, we'd only won twice in the league at Meadow Park. Suddenly everything came together that day with comprehensive 7-0 win. A hat trick from Morias, and goals from Reynolds, Montgomery, Oyenuga and substitute Lee Angol sealed Tonbridge's fate. Oyenuga even had the bottle to take the ball off Assistant Manager Luke Garrard to take a penalty, which he subsequently missed! A few days later the rearranged match at home to Havant and Waterlooville resulted in a disappointing 2-0 defeat. We followed that up with another comprehensive win against Dorchester, this time 4-1 away. While at the Maidenhead United away game the following Tuesday, it was pointed out by one of our supporters that we hadn't won a midweek away game in the league for just over three years. This was quite remarkable bearing in mind the amount of games we had played in that time. This was a gripping encounter in which the home team looked like snatching it. But for some great saves by James Russell they would have done. However with almost the last kick of the game Junior Morias scored an excellent winner sending the supporters into raptures as they celebrated this good fortune with the players. This joint celebration was memorable and would be repeated several times over the next twelve months or so. Our midweek away day hoodoo was over. I was now in the zone where I didn't want to miss a game. We still had plenty left to play.

The following Saturday, Harry and I took almost every mode of transport possible to go to Gosport Borough away. We travelled by car, tube, train, boat and bus to make the game. (Surely an airplane and helicopter are the only things left). There was a carnival atmosphere at "Privett Park" that day as Gosport Borough were a week away from playing in the FA Trophy Final at Wembley and the whole place was buzzing. Harry and I even had to leave our seats at half time because Gosport had a massive flag they wanted to put across all the seats. This flag was the biggest I've ever seen and had been donated to the club by a local company in recognition of their Wembley appearance. I did the right thing and helped them put it across the seats. I got ribbed constantly by some Boreham Wood supporters for this afterwards. I came so close to buying tickets for the Cup Final myself but thought better of it. Although the home team's mind may have been on the cup final you wouldn't have known it as they dominated the match and went 2-0 up with two goals from hotshot Justin Bennett. However, the introduction of Junior Morias from the bench with five minutes to go changed the game as he scored one and should have got a second in injury time. We were left disappointed with a 2-1 defeat even though the right team won. After the match Harry and I had a bit of a race on to get the 5:20pm train from Portsmouth. If we missed it, the next train was at 6:50pm so we had to hurry. Basically we had to rely on the bus coming within two minutes, which it did. We then had to rely on the Gosport Ferry leaving as soon as we got there, which it did. At that point we had an agonising five minute walk to the platform which had to done in four minutes, which it was!! Somehow we got on the train. I was extremely out of breath by this stage so welcomed the seat and the one and a half hour rest while the train sped back to Waterloo. I remember thinking, I'll drive next year.

The following week was crucial with three massive games. On the Monday night we drew 1-1 at home to relegation rivals Farnborough with an excellent Noto free kick securing a point. This turned out to be Mario Noto's last goal for Boreham Wood. For the previous couple of years Noto started to appear less for the club. Perhaps some of the injuries he had were taking their toll. However his role as First Team Coach was increasingly invaluable to our success. On the Thursday night Baz and I drove to Canvey Island to watch us play at Concord Rangers. On paper this was a hard game played in poor conditions at a substandard ground. Who the bloody hell plays on a Thursday night anyway? The result in this match all but secured our safety in the Conference South. More significantly it highlighted the quality of Lee Angol. Angol had been a substitute more often than not since joining the club. Following his performance that night he was never left on the bench again. Concord couldn't live with him. Although Angol didn't get on the scoresheet, defender Cameron Mawer did, as did Reynolds and Junior Morias (twice). The 4-0 win was confirmed by a quite brilliant Morias goal at the end which was in my opinion the best goal we scored all season. We followed that up with a 2-1 win at home to Ebbsfleet on the Saturday with Angol deservedly on the scoresheet.

At the Maidenhead match it became apparent that there was no Charlie O'Loughlin in the starting line-up. It wasn't unusual because O'Loughlin now a trained Architect had occasionally missed matches because of studies and travel etc.. When O'Loughlin missed the following games against Gosport and Farnborough, questions were being asked. It was soon revealed the he had accepted a job in Uzbekistan which was apparently going to earn him a vast fortune but he had to start it straight away. It was a disappointing way to end his three years at the club but I understand he had to look after himself. The supporter's initial disappointment was fairly short lived especially as his replacement Josh Hill signed from Dartford, made an impressive start against Ebbsfleet. We soon realised that we didn't really miss Charlie O'Loughlin that much after all. Hill would be easily as good but without the disciplinary problems to go with it. Sam Cox took over O'Loughlin's role as Captain.

Something's Gotten Hold Of My "Hert"

The Herts Senior Cup (or the Hertfordshire County Football Association Senior Challenge Cup to give it its proper title) is the oldest county based cup competition in the country having started in 1886. The county Headquarters are based at The County Ground, Letchworth where the bigwigs at the County FA insist that their Cup Final should be held despite other County Cup finals taking place at more exotic locations. (For example the 2015 Sussex County Cup final was held at The Amex Stadium, Brighton). This is partly the reason why the The Herts Senior Cup is often not considered important. If the showpiece final was held at Vicarage Road, Watford or even The Lamex Stadium, Stevenage there would surely be more interest. I attended my first Boreham Wood match in 2008 just four days after we won the trophy against Ware and I knew nothing about it. There was no open top bus parade, no showing off of the trophy before the game and no mention of it among the supporters I spoke to that day. Our performances in the competition since 2008 had left a lot to be desired. We'd often got knocked out to lower division opposition and no one seemed to care.

However in the 2013-14 season things were slightly different. We managed to overcome Berkhamsted Town away 3-2 in early December and we all seemed to forget about it. However during our enormous fixture pile up we had a quarter final to play at home to Watford on 25th March. By this time we were virtually safe from relegation so why not give it a go? This match against a Watford side made up of youth and reserve team players marked the long awaited debut for Ricky Shakes who had been injured all season. With a maximum of twelve matches left of our season, Shakes now had a chance to make an impact and earn a new contract for the following year. We beat Watford 2-0 with goals from Morias and Whichelow.

The gap between the previous round against Berkhamsted and the Watford match was three months. The gap between the quarter final and the semi-final was two days!! This was supposed to be the team's only week off before the end of the season and they ended up playing two midweek matches. On the Thursday night I went to Hitchin to watch the semi-final with a place against Bishops Stortford in the final at stake. Our preparation for the match wasn't great. This was the clubs tenth competitive match in just over three weeks and there were a number of regulars missing. As well as that, defender Cameron Mawer (who had been named in the starting line-up) arrived at the ground two minutes before kick off as he'd been held up at a coaching course. Despite all these obstacles, a Lee Angol goal secured a hard fought 1-0 win and a place at Letchworth!!

The final against Bishop's Stortford was held on Wednesday 23rd April and because of the school holidays, five year old Harry was there for his first ever night match. The ground was shocking and surely not the right place to host a Senior Cup Final. I wouldn't even host the final of tiddlywinks there! The match was a cracker though and the performance of the team that night was exceptional. Sitting among us was Junior Morias we'd recently returned to Wycombe Wanderers to assist in their League Two relegation fight. It was his Wycombe team mate Lee Angol who scored a fantastic goal after two minutes to give us the lead. A Stortford equalizer soon afterwards made it 1-1 and when Stortford were reduced to ten men just after the hour mark we were the only team who looked like winning it. We continued our dominance by having a number of chances and hitting the post four times. As the match went into extra time Harry was starting to feel all of his five years old by constantly moaning about how tired he was and that he wanted to go home. It was Sod's law that his first night match ends in extra time and penalties making a late night even later. With the help of Linda and Gill Cox (Sam Cox's mum who was sitting next to us) Harry perked up and by the time we got to the penalty shootout he was excited and talking non-stop.

My record as a supporter in penalty shoot outs was appalling. Being an England supporter we have a history of going out of tournaments in such circumstances. As for Spurs, the 1984 UEFA Cup Final win against Anderlecht will live long in the memory. The two or three penalty shootout wins we've had since meant bugger all as they had been in cup competitions where we've gone out in the following round anyway. This night at Letchworth my mind went back to Euro 1996 and the shootout defeat to Germany at Wembley in the Semi-Final. That was heartbreaking and only beaten in that respects by the 1990 World Cup defeat. Former Spurs player Stefan Freund had been in the Germany line up that night at Wembley. Sitting in front of me at Letchworth alongside our Reserve Team Manager Kevin Lucas was Niklas Freund, Stefan's son and Boreham Wood reserve goalkeeper. He was a really nice chap who had been an excellent goalkeeper for our second team all season and as well as that, always seemed to be at our first team matches when the reserves weren't playing. He was a popular figure around the club.

Perhaps having a German among the staff would rub off on our team when it came to the penalty shootouts. This certainly had an effect when James Russell saved their first penalty. Up stepped Callum Reynolds for our first penalty. I asked why he was taking it and was told by Kevin Lucas "he always scored them in training". To prove Kevin's point Reynolds buried his spot kick to give us the lead. Stortford scored their next penalty before right back Ben Nunn stepped up. I again asked why he was taking it. (It's strange for a centre half and a right back to be the first two penalty takers). I was given the same answer by Kevin Lucas. Low and behold Ben Nunn also buried his spot kick. I decided to shut up after that and leave the football to the experts!! Former Boreham Wood forward Cliff Akurang then had his penalty saved by Russell before Lee Angol made it 3-1 from the spot. The equation was now simple. Luke Milbourne had to score the next penalty for Stortford or the cup would belong to Boreham Wood. Again James Russell dived to pull off a great save to win the cup for Boreham Wood. The usual jumping on the goalkeeper by all the players occurred. The impressive turnout of Boreham Wood supporters went berserk. Harry was in his element and loving the occasion. The team collected their trophy and medals in a mood of celebration. It was only the Herts Senior Cup but in my opinion this gave the team a taste of glory that would come in handy twelve months later. The cup win would help secure our fantastic team spirit which would be invaluable with all the challenges that lay ahead.

After the match a few supporters went back to the bar at the club. I had a disagreement with Harry as he wanted to join us. He'd gone from being desperate to go home at 9:45pm to wanting to go to the bar at 10:30pm!! After much debate I dropped him home and put him to bed before Linda and I went for a drink. Someone brought the trophy in and left it up on the bar. For about twenty minutes the oldest county cup competition trophy in England was just sitting there without anyone giving it a second glance. I picked it up and had loads of photos taken with it. It was a pleasant atmosphere at the club, not scenes of jubilant celebration but acknowledgement of a job well done. The scenes of jubilant celebrations, could wait another twelve months.

With the Herts Senior Cup in 2014

Come Together

With all the excitement of the Herts Senior Cup win, we still had a league programme to complete. Following our 2-1 victory our Ebbsfleet in March we went to Dover Athletic for another hard fought contest against the promotion chasers from Kent. I didn't rate Dover at all. We were unlucky not to come away with a better result than 0-0. Dover supporters were on their manager's back and disappointed at the way they were playing. It was therefore a surprise that Dover having managed to sneak into the play offs, went on to win at hot favourites Ebbsfleet United in the Promotion Final to take their place in the Conference National for the 2014-15 season. I've no doubt we were a better team than Dover by March 2014. If they could do it, so could we.

At the beginning of April we lost 1-0 at Sutton United which was followed up by probably the most entertaining match of the season. Two goals each from Lee Angol and Matty Whichelow secured a 4-3 win against Chelmsford with Whichelow's second the pick of the bunch. Whichelow has struggled for form and fitness during his first few months at the club but was now starting to turn it on. This was followed up by a 3-1 win against promotion chasers Eastbourne Borough. The following Saturday it was the turn of Whitehawk to make their first appearance at Meadow Park. The Sussex side had a number of new players side since we last played them. They also had a new manager in Steve King as Darren Freeman who had led them up the leagues had been sacked. Despite these changes, Whitehawk were still in the relegation mire. They would eventually survive relegation on the last day of the season. Before the game there'd been a lot of talk among supporters about who should be "Player of the Year". I told anyone who would listen that it should be Sam Cox. There were many reasons for this but I kept highlighting his disciplinary record outlining that he was "never booked and never sent off". However after thirty-four minutes Cox was sent off!! I naturally got a load of stick for "tempting fate", however I was safe in the knowledge that it was a ridiculous decision as he was given an "early bath" for a handball in the penalty area when it wasn't a goalscoring opportunity. Whitehawk scored from the resulting penalty and went on to win 3-1.

We followed this up on the Wednesday night with Ricky Shakes scoring his first Boreham Wood goal in a 1-1 draw at Havant & Waterlooville. Shakes was starting to look like the player we'd signed before his injury. On Easter Saturday the Lewis family managed to combine a day out at Thorpe Park with Hayes & Yeading away at Woking FC in the afternoon. The female members of the family went to Woking Shopping Centre while Harry and I went to the game. By this time, Junior Morias had been recalled by Wycombe and we missed him. We were poor that day and lost 1-0 to a late goal. Hayes who were desperate for points at the bottom celebrated wildly. Unfortunately for them, they were relegated although later reprieved due to the demise of Hereford United. The Hayes & Yeading defeat was followed up by yet another loss against Staines Town, going down 2-0 at home on Bank Holiday Monday.

Despite losing three times in four league matches, spirits were high following our Herts Senior Cup victory as we went into our final match of the season away at league champions Eastleigh. Eastleigh had already collected their trophy at a previous home game. An entertaining match was settled by a Greg Morgan goal to give us a well-deserved 1-0 win. Beating the champions away represented an excellent way to finish a season that started off poorly and ended very well. Although our thirteenth place finish was disappointing, I don't think it reflected the quality of the squad we had by the end of the season. I felt that if we could keep these players together the following season we would be at the "business end" of the league table. I knew we would keep most of the squad but felt that keeping Lee Angol and possibly getting Junior Morias back was crucial to our chances. It occurred to me that with Wycombe now knowing what these two were capable off that this seemed unlikely.

The Herts Senior Cup Final win 2014 gave the club a taste of success

2014-2015 SEASON

Here Comes the Summer

The summer of 2014 was an exciting one. Unfortunately this wasn't because of the World Cup as England's showing in the competition in Brazil was our worst World Cup performance since 1958 as we failed to get out of the group. While the nation was going through the two-yearly inquest as to "what went wrong", things were much brighter for Boreham Wood FC.

Off the pitch, the fantastic new West Stand was ready and waiting for its "grand opening" at the pre-season match against Arsenal on 19th July. The PASE Academy had an excellent summer with the opening of the site at the Old Elizabethan Training Complex in Barnet which would vastly improve the scope of the PASE Scheme.

On the pitch, James Russell, James Courtnage (number 2 goalkeeper), Ben Nunn, Josh Hill, Callum Reynolds, Mario Noto, Graeme Montgomery, Luke Garrard, Greg Morgan, Matty Whichelow and Ricky Shakes all signed new contracts before the previous season had even finished. Sam Cox did eventually sign by the time the pre-season matches were in full flow. However, significantly his delay in re-signing meant the captaincy for the 2014-15 season was handed to Callum Reynolds. We said goodbye to Mark Jones who after three years great service and a number of years previously at Braintree, decided to hang up his boots. Combative midfielder Scott Thomas joined from Chesham United and Arsenal forward Austin Lipman rejoined on a season long loan. The best news of all came in early July when the re-signing of Lee Angol was announced. Angol had been released by Wycombe Wanderers and was snapped up by Luton Town on a twelve month contract only to be loaned back to Boreham Wood for the whole season. I'm not sure what Luton's plans were long term for Lee Angol but it was great news that our club managed to secure this deal which was no doubt helped by the great relationship between our club and Luton Town Manager John Still. I felt that with Lee Angol in our squad, anything was possible. Unfortunately for us, at this stage we couldn't secure a deal for his strike colleague Junior Morias as he signed a new contract with Wycombe Wanderers. Having the two of them together would have been too much to ask but I was confident that Angol would work well with Austin Lipman upfront. As for the rest of the squad I felt they could carry on where they left off. Defender Josh Hill had been impressive since joining the club as a replacement for Charlie O'Loughlin. Ricky Shakes had been excellent since returning from injury in March and having him fully fit would make a huge difference to the team. As well as that, Matty Whichelow who had struggled at the beginning of the 2013-14 season ended the season in great form so was raring to go.

There were some areas of concern though. Mark Jones hadn't been replaced so Greg Morgan was filling in at left back. Although he didn't do a bad job there, I felt we would need an experienced left back to carry us through. Right back Ben Nunn had committed to going travelling to Australia and would be missing between September and the end of February. This is a hell of a long time to be without the best right back in the Conference South. Although Luke Garrard would fill in, it is ironic that it took until the time Ben Nunn returned to find a right back equally as good as him, to solve our left back problem!! More about that later. Despite these concerns I was really looking forward to the 2014-2015 season.

It's worth pointing out that playing pre-season matches against Boreham Wood was a lucky omen for league clubs during this period. In the summer of 2014 the teams we'd played had experienced very good seasons either side of these fixtures. For example, Brentford had just been promoted to the Championship after twenty two years in what is now Leagues One and League Two. Amazingly they went on to make the Championship play offs in 2014-15. Arsenal had just won the FA Cup and would do so again in 2015. Luton Town and Cambridge United had just been promoted to the Football League and Watford were promoted to the Premier League in 2015. This a stark message to other clubs out there. If you want to have a successful season, then it's good to arrange a pre-season friendly with Boreham Wood!!

The busy pre-season programme started on 17th July at home against Brentford. Former Boreham Wood player and then Brentford Manager Mark Warburton had a full strength team on show that night and the visitors went on to win 3-1 despite a good performance from Boreham Wood. Two days later it was the turn of the showpiece match against Arsenal at home. This was a significant match as it heralded the opening of our new West Stand by Arsene Wenger which cemented the relationship between the two clubs. Arsenal brought their strongest possible squad though without any of their World Cup players who were still on holiday. While I acknowledge the strong relationship between the clubs I can't say I was looking forward to the fixture. Normally pre-season matches between the clubs have gates of between five hundred and a thousand people, usually made up of local Arsenal supporters who were happy to see their youth team play as it's ten minutes from home. This day was quite different though. There would be a crowd of three and a half thousand to watch Arsenal's first team with probably no more than two hundred Boreham Wood supporters present. In other words I had to spend two hours in the same ground as thousands of them which didn't sit well with me. No more than thirty seconds after entering the ground, an Arsenal supporter said something to me and I told him to "piss off". I can't remember what he said but it was annoying. For whatever reason this act of belligerence against a mouthy Arsenal fan made me feel slightly better about being there. The match itself wasn't particularly memorable as Boreham Wood hardly touched the ball although Arsenal didn't create much. Eventually two second half goals from the away team resulted in a 2-0 defeat for Boreham Wood. The match was mostly memorable for a fantastic turn and cross field pass from Graeme Montgomery that was worth the £22 admission fee alone. Montgomery went on to be "untouchable" in the first part of the season. The second Arsenal goal was scored from the spot by youngster, Benik Afobe, who was to have an interesting next couple of years. Afobe had been at Arsenal for many years progressing though their youth structure having started in the Under 9s playing upfront alongside a kid called Harry Kane (Arsenal in their wisdom decided that young Kane wasn't good enough and the rest as they say is history, ha ha!). A few months after the Boreham Wood Vs Arsenal fixture, Afobe was part of the Milton Keynes Dons side that famously beat Manchester United 4-0 in the Second Round of the League Cup, coming off the bench to score twice. Following a successful year at Wolves, he joined Premier League Bournemouth in January 2016 for a staggering fee of £10million. I'm convinced, it all started for him on that hot summers day in Borehamwood. No doubt he'll look back on his contribution that day against a stout Boreham Wood defence as one of the finest achievements of his career!!

The following Tuesday night we drew 0-0 against Cambridge and two days later hosted a very strong Watford team although they were without Troy Deeney. The rumour among Watford fans was that their talismanic striker was about to be sold hence his non-appearance. It turned out he had been injured and was going nowhere. We gave a good account of ourselves that night and only lost 1-0. Twenty four hours later we were back in action against a Reading X1 in a 0-0 draw. The following Tuesday we played out another 0-0 draw against Luton Town. We rounded off our pre-season against an Arsenal X1 (a similar Gunners team that normally comes to Meadow Park) and played out an excellent 2-2 draw.

Soon after the fixtures for the 2014-2015 season were announced, Salisbury City who had already been relegated to the Conference South from the Conference National due to financial problems were thrown out of the Conference all together. Apparently a "rich Arabic owner" who had no money came in with plenty of fanfare and bled them dry. It makes me laugh when supporters get excited about new foreign owners, automatically assuming they have another Roman Abramovich and it all ends in tears. In the summer of 2014 Salisbury City supporters were throwing themselves at the mercy of the league but the club had failed to contact the league in the first place to inform them of a change of ownership. Sadly a great non-league institution like Salisbury City with a large fan base, had no league to play in during the 2014-15 as all the fixtures had been released. Unfortunately this reduced the Conference South from 22 to 21 teams therefore reducing the amount of league fixtures from 42 to 40. Each club would therefore have two free Saturdays in the season when they would have played Salisbury. The whole thing was a farce and should have been dealt with by then.

It Started With a Kiss

On 9th August 2014 the best football season of my life was underway. It started with an absolute masterclass and despite a few hiccups along the way, continued like that for the rest of an incredible season. It was a season where I couldn't wait for the next game. I thought about football all the time, when I should have been thinking about other things. The only time I missed any matches during the 2014-15 season were because of stag do's, weddings, a weekend away, Yom Kippur (Jewish Festival) and a prior arrangement to watch the fabulous PP Arnold live at the 100 Club. Apart from that, I was at every match. Apart from a stroppy fit which caused Harry to miss the Staines Town match early on, he came to every game he could, apart from on school nights. He even went to one match I didn't go to!! This was the season that Harry really caught the bug. He would spend hours looking at match day programmes and watch a number of Boreham Wood games on YouTube. He would begin to recognize all the players, remember incidents in matches, directions to matches, things I'd long since forgotten. At the end of the season Harry like the rest of us, experienced an incredible high. During the season, we scored nearly a hundred goals and were top of the table for most of it even though we were thrashed a few times. It didn't matter too much because it's better to lose a match 4-0 then four matches 1-0. We missed out on the title by two points to Bromley, eventually having to settle for second place and the play offs.

Sometimes you get a moment that will stay with you for ever. For me it might be the first time I saw the full length live performance of the *Lynyrd Skynyrd* song "Freebird" on "The

Old Grey Whistle Test" (some years after it happened – I'm not that old!!) or Gazza's free kick in the FA Cup semi-final against Arsenal. I may sound dramatic but on 9th August 2014 at Meadow Park we witnessed such a moment courtesy of Boreham Wood's Graeme Montgomery. What happened in the first ten minutes of that match wasn't just worth the admission money but the season ticket money!! After two minutes Monty hit a volley from thirty yards (that came from a high ball played from the right) across the goalkeeper into the far corner of the goal. He never took his eye off it. It was a technique that belonged four divisions higher. This is surely the best goal ever scored at Meadow Park and I know I'm biased but it was surely one of the best goal scored in the country in the 2014-15 season. After nine minutes Montgomery produced something that was even better. He received the ball from Josh Hill with his back to goal and within an instance took a couple of touches, turned and hit a shot that had the keeper beaten and hit the underside of the bar. This would have been a better goal then the first one and would have made James Rodriquez goal for Columbia against Uruguay at the recent World Cup look like a tap in. Lee Angol added a second goal after fourteen minutes and Boreham Wood secured a convincing 2-0 victory.

A few days later we were away to Hemel Hempstead. Hemel had just been promoted to the Conference South having won the Southern League convincingly in the 2013-14 season. Harry accompanied me to his first ever night league match. For the first thirty minutes it was clear that the home team were no push over with Jordan Parkes particularly impressive. They were the better team and Boreham Wood looked lethargic and lacking in ideas. However, after thirty-four minutes an excellent goal by Lee Angol against the run of play gave Boreham Wood the lead. Just before half time Graeme Montgomery added the second from a tight angle. The 2-0 lead at half time was flattering. A minute after the restart Austin Lipman finished well to make it 3-0 after a fine through ball from Lee Angol. Hemel Hempstead were shell shocked and we started to dominate. All it took were three great finishes either side of half time and the game was over as a contest. A year earlier we had Donovan Simmonds up front and an out of form Graeme Montgomery. Now we had Lee Angol up front and an "out of this world" Graeme Montgomery. After seventy minutes, Lee Angol added a fourth following a mistake in the Hemel defence (which he'd engineered) and on seventy five minutes we scored the goal of the match. Again it was Montgomery who scored it. He chipped the ball over the keeper from twenty five yards in the far corner. There was only one place it could have gone in and due to Monty's accuracy, he found it. I was standing behind the goal at the time and saw it at a perfect angle. I wish I'd filmed it as it was a great moment. Matty Whichelow added a sixth a few minutes later. The 6-0 win at Hemel was a statement of intent. I tweeted Hemel Hempstead Football Club the following morning to ask if the match had been filmed. I got a response two days later with the YouTube link. I couldn't stop watching it over the next few days.

After two matches we were top of the league not that league positions really mattered at this stage of the season. The next match was away at Staines Town. We had failed to beat Staines in the last fifteen matches but surely this would be the day we end the hoodoo. The day started badly as the usual forty five minute journey took over two hours due to traffic on the "road to hell" (M25). We arrived just before kick-off. Unfortunately the Boreham Wood players arrived four minutes later as I'm not quite sure what they were doing for the first three minutes of the match. By that time we were already 2-0 down. It took a while to get going and when Callum Reynolds header reduced the arrears after half an hour, we looked like we'd go on and win it. Unfortunately the score remained 2-1 and we lost our first match of the season. Staines Town were a funny side that season. They went down with only twenty five points but managed to beat both Boreham Wood at home and eventual champions Bromley away.

Unfortunately I missed the following two matches played over the August Bank Holiday weekend as we had a family weekend in The Cotswolds. In the first of these matches we played out a 1-1 draw against Bromley. We took the lead soon after half time with another wonder strike from Montgomery only to be undone by a late equalizer in a game we should have won. This result was significant come the end of the season. On the Bank Holiday Monday we were away to Sutton United, a fixture that we never seemed to win. I was annoyed because I could have gone to this match had Paula not wanted to go to a factory outlet in Swindon on our way home!! She ended up buying things she could have bought at Brent Cross or Watford anyway. That's women for you!! Sutton led until three late goals including two in injury time secured a fabulous 3-1 win for Boreham Wood. The following Saturday it was the turn of Bath City to come to Meadow Park. We fully expected to win this game because we were sitting comfortably in second place and Bath City only had a solitary point from their first five matches. With this in mind I persuaded my friend Scott to come to the game as I wanted him to see how good we were. I'm not sure what happened that day but we were outclassed from start to finish. The team we'd watched in the first five matches just didn't show up. Despite all the visitors' dominance, we took the lead with Scott Thomas's first goal for the club after twenty three minutes. However two goals either side of half time won the match for Bath. The second goal came from an excellent little player called Ross Stearn who's often been Boreham Wood's nemesis while at Bath and Weston Super Mare previously. My mate Scott was suitably unimpressed as was a woman in the crowd when Barry accused the Bath City left back of cheating. This created a bit of an exchange between Baz and the woman. At the end of the game the angry Bath left back came up to me and accused me of having a go at his mum!! Although this was a case of mistaken identity, this wasn't the first Baz time had failed to endear himself to a visiting player's family at a football match. Barry, bless him, has a habit of "expressing himself".

Get Yourself Together

Next up was another trip to Gosport Borough. This time I took a less complicated journey and drove there. We were playing a very good Gosport team who were unbeaten. This fixture took place on "Non-League Day". This initiative had been set up a few years earlier to highlight non-league football when there were no fixtures in the Premier League and Championship due to the international break. Clubs at this level tend to offer a promotion to supporters to get more people to attend. Arsenal FC very kindly gave Boreham Wood players and officials the use of their team coach for the match therefore saving the club a lot of money in transport costs.. My cheeky attempt to get a seat on the coach was rightly refused. I found out the day before that Gosport were offering free entry to all Premier League and Football League season ticket holders, servicemen and women and anybody with VAN in their names!! I fitted none of the criteria until my Arsenal supporting boss lent me his season ticket. Before making a "pact with the devil" I'd explored all options of changing my name to Brett Van Lewis (or having a sex change) but neither were feasible options at such short notice. I took the season ticket and hoped that no one asked me anything. Pride is one thing but £14 is better in my pocket than theirs. The match was a tense affair, similar to some of the matches later in the season. Although we didn't play badly I thought Gosport were the better team on the day. However the match was settled by a deadly finish from Lee Angol on fifty-eight minutes despite the home team having a number of chances. It was a real backs to the wall effort. There was a mood of celebration at the end from the players and the ten or so away supporters who bothered to make the trip.

Two days later we were back in action at home against Eastbourne Borough. The Sussex side were the early pace setters, unbeaten and one point clear of Boreham Wood so this promised to be a real ding dong encounter. The match lived up to its billing. It had everything and was definitely one of the best matches I'd ever seen Boreham Wood involved in. After fourteen minutes we were already 3-1 up with another world class goal from Graeme Montgomery the pick of them. This genius with a magic wand of a left foot was winning his own goal of the season competition. He was giving Boreham Wood supporters memories that would stay with them forever. Other goals from Lipman (2), Angol and Whichelow secured a fantastic 5-2 win. I'll remember the match for other reasons too. At half time with his team 3-1 down Eastbourne manager Tommy Widdrington forcefully came up to have a pop at us, allegedly because of something Baz may have said. His strong North East accent made him sound more aggressive than he was. While being restrained by the steward, Widdrington lashed out at him. Although it probably looked worse than it was, this caused a mêlée. By the time the Eastbourne players came out for the second half, Widdrington (probably feeling a bit silly) had been sent to the stand. Football can be a passionate game, especially when you have players like Montgomery scoring goals like he was scoring at the time.

The following Saturday I went to my friend Kieron's wedding in Cornwall so missed the Chelmsford match at home. While I was sipping Pimms and a variety other drinks at the fantastic setting of "The Green" near Bodmin Moor, Boreham Wood won their third league match in a row, this time 4-0. An own goal, two penalties by Garrard and another goal by Angol secured the points. At this time a new striker arrived. I'd hoped it was Junior Morias who had recently been released by Wycombe and was playing for the QPR Under 21's team. However it was David Moli instead. Moli had been released by Wolves and was a free agent. I hoped we'd see a better David Moli than a year earlier. Unfortunately despite a promising start he was disappointing again. Next up was a crucial away game at Basingstoke Town. We were top of the table with the Hampshire side in fifth place. We were excellent in the first half and should have had a penalty early on when Basingstoke defender Jay Gasson was practicing for a game of volley ball in the penalty area. Unfortunately the referee didn't see it. The outstanding Ricky Shakes eased the nerves soon afterwards by giving us the lead. The second half was more even with the home team now creating chances. The equalizer came after fifty-eight minutes and with six minutes left came a significant moment. David Moli hit a fantastic shot towards the far corner of the net which somehow the keeper managed to push away. I was prematurely celebrating a goal. Basingstoke predictably went straight up the other end and scored the winner. This was heartbreaking for the Boreham Wood team and the travelling supporters. We were the better side only to be undone by a sucker punch. A draw would have been a good result but having tried to get the winner we ended up losing. This naivety would cost us a few times that season, especially against our promotion rivals.

The Basingstoke match was the last we'd see of Ben Nunn until late February. He had a long standing arrangement to go travelling soon after the Basingstoke match. What a difference it would have made to have Nunn for the whole season. I'm sure we'd have more than made up the eventual two point gap behind Bromley with him in the side. The plan was to have Luke Garrard as a replacement while Nunn was away. Unfortunately Garrard wasn't as good as Ben Nunn, although still a good defender, Garrard didn't have his pace to go up and down the line. This is no reflection on Luke Garrard but Nunn was the best right back in the division.

We were drawn against East Preston in the Second Qualifying Round of the FA Cup. It took me a while to realize that East Preston wasn't a place in Lancashire but a small village near Littlehampton in Sussex. They were doing well in the Sussex League and came to Boreham Wood on 27th September to cause an upset and very nearly achieved it. There was no sign of what was to come when Lee Angol gave Boreham Wood the lead after twenty four minutes. However after fifty two minutes East Preston were 2-1 up with goals either side of half time. The Sussex side held on but with twelve minutes to go Angol scored again to make it 2-2. On the eighty fourth minute Greg Morgan scored the winner and Meadow Park breathed a huge sigh of relief.

Prior to the next match, another table topper at Havant & Waterlooville, we signed left back Jordan Browne from Bishops Stortford to fill the void left by Mark Jones departure at the end of the previous season. I missed the Havant match as it was the Jewish festival, Yom Kippur. However by all accounts it was similar to the Basingstoke match. We took an early lead only to lose 2-1. With the clock ticking down, Lee

Angol who had already been booked was apparently fouled in the penalty area. However the referee thought he dived so gave Angol a second yellow card, sending him off rather than giving us a penalty. This was to be one of only two sending offs we have all season. No disrespect, but with the departures of Charlie O'Loughlin and Mark Jones who were always likely to get send off at odd times, our disciplinary record in the 2014-15 season was exemplary. Our injury record was particularly good too, due to some good fortune and great work by the club physiotherapists.

Two days after the Havant match we were at home to local rivals St Albans who had just been promoted back to the Conference South via the Southern League Play Off Final. On the morning of the St Albans match, Boreham Wood supporters got the news they'd been waiting for. Junior Morias re-joined the club on a permanent basis to reform his strike partnership with former Wycombe teammate and close friend Lee Angol. This was fantastic news as everyone fully expected the partnership to yield plenty of goals. With the score 1-1 in a tightly fought encounter against a very good St Albans team, Morias made his entrance from the bench on the hour mark. Predictably he scored an excellent winner after seventy-eight minutes to give us a 2-1 victory to mark his second debut for the club. There was a great derby atmosphere at Meadow Park that night and a realization that with Morias's return we were definitely in with a very good chance of promotion. This victory put Boreham Wood top of the table ahead of Havant & Waterlooville on goal difference.

The following Saturday we were away at Frome Town in the Third Qualifying Round of the FA Cup. Only twenty four hours earlier I had my wisdom teeth out so was feeling a bit tender. Fortunately Barry volunteered to drive us. The Somerset side, two divisions below us, were more than a match for Boreham Wood. We managed to come from behind twice to draw 2-2 with goals from Montgomery and Morias. However we were lucky to hold out at the end. The replay was only two days later at Meadow Park. The replay was played in horrendous conditions with heavy rain dictating the quality of the contest. The expected drubbing didn't materialize and if anything, Frome played better than they did two days before. Fortunately a Lee Angol goal settled the tie and we marched on to the next round. This victory set up a Fourth Qualifying Round tie at Conference National side Woking two weeks later. The Woking match turned out to be pulsating encounter with Boreham Wood giving as good as they got. For the first time this season Lee Angol didn't have his shooting boots on. Had he done we'd have been 2-0 up before Giuseppe Sole gave Woking the lead on fifty six minutes. However a minute later a great Montgomery cross was turned in by Ricky Shakes for a deserved equalizer. Unfortunately moments later the dangerous Sole scored again to put Woking back in front. In the last minute David Moli headed home to send the Boreham Wood supporters in raptures however a linesman correctly ruled it out for offside. Unfortunately that was it and Woking went into the First Round. This was another honourable defeat in the FA Cup. We could concentrate on the league and hopefully a decent FA Trophy run.

The week after the Frome match, we played the first of two matches that season at Maidenhead United's York Road ground. New tenants Hayes & Yeading were still without a ground of their own and following the end of a ground share agreement with Woking, agreed a similar deal with Maidenhead United. There were strong rumours at the time that Hayes & Yeading were running out of money and would no longer be in existence by Christmas. The building of the new ground has long since been postponed and it was sad to see such non-league institutions like Hayes FC and Yeading FC (now merged) in such trouble. The attendance of only two hundred and fifty gave every indication that the supporters were slowly giving up on the club. Obviously our usual poor away attendance of about half a dozen didn't help. Despite Lee Angol being suspended, it was a very one sided 3-0 victory. In fact if we had Angol playing rather than David Moli, it would have been six or seven easily!! To help matters Hayes were reduced to nine men after two sending's off. Goals from Garrard, Morias and Whichelow saw us comfortingly home. Unfortunately Basingstoke Town's injury time winner at Wealdstone on the same day meant they would go above us at the top of the league.

I've Got a Feeling

We then had a two week break as Saturday 1st November was the day we were supposed to play Salisbury. Fortunately for me, that was the weekend I'd decided to take Paula on a surprise trip to Las Vegas for her fortieth birthday. As I booked this some months before, I wouldn't have known about the Salisbury situation. This good fortune I had was shared with the team when we played Wealdstone on the 8th November at Meadow Park. For years Wealdstone had been knocking on the door of promotion from the Ryman League and Gordon Bartlett's side eventually won the league in 2013-14 by eleven points. The visitors took an early lead and with their goalie Jonathan North in fine form we failed to score from the numerous chances we created. Towards the end of the match the heavens opened and on the eighty-seventh minute Angol equalized. At this point, I've have taken 1-1 having been behind for seventy five minutes of the match. However Sam Cox had other ideas and came up with a rare goal with the last kick of the game to win it. This was harsh on Weald-stone but over the ninety minutes, we deserved it. A mood of celebrating followed in the heavy rain. Late winners are always good for team spirit. Two days later we were at home against Maidenhead United. Again, the visitors took the lead this time just before half time, again it started raining late on and again Angol equalized this time on seventy six minutes only for Junior Morias to score another late winner. The rain had made lightning strike twice! With two late winners in three days we were now four points clear of Basingstoke at the top of the league.

After all this fun and games, we were away at Concord Rangers the following Saturday. Before the match we took a drive to Canvey Island seafront around the corner from the ground. On surveying the "destruction", it's hard to believe that that this was Britain's most popular seaside town until 1921. I'm sure since then it must have been overtaken by every other seaside town in the UK!! Perhaps it would have looked better during the summer. Unfortunately Concord's Thames Road ground wasn't much better. The previous time I'd been there was for an evening match so this was the first time I'd seen the large caravan park along the side of the pitch behind where the dugouts are. From a distance they looked extremely grotty and wouldn't have been out of place in the Guy Richie film "Snatch". I certainly wouldn't have taken part in a bare knuckle boxing match to try and get one. Our excel-lent form leading up to this match gave me every indication that we would win. However I hadn't taken into account the usual fighting spirit of Danny Cowley's team. We took the lead just after the half hour mark with a Montgomery goal. This wasn't in the running for goal of the century like his others that season but it was a tidy finish nonetheless. We looked in control and Angol should have finished the match just before the hour mark when he just about failed to get on the end of a Morias cross. This was a turning point and from then on, it was all Concord. Soon afterwards the impressive Jordan Chiedozie equalized and the home team had a number of chances to win it. In the end we were lucky to hold out for a draw. Around the time of the fixture, Concord were in the middle of a great FA Cup run. Prior to our match, they had secured an excellent 1-1 draw at League Two Mansfield Town in the First Round with Chiedozie scoring a cracking equalizer with the goal being shown again and again on the BBC. The replay took place four days before we played Concord Rangers again (two weeks after the league match) at Thames Road. Unfortunately we were drawn against them in the third qualifying round of the FA Trophy. Before we played them again, we had two league matches to negotiate. The first of these was at home to Gosport Borough on 22nd November. We had to settle for a Ricky Shakes equalizer to secure a 1-1 draw in a match we should have won. Two days later we did win, convincingly 4-0 at home to bottom club Weston Super Mare with two goals each from Montgomery and Angol. We opened up a six point gap at the top of the Conference South albeit with teams around us having games in hand.

The fact we had to play Concord Rangers again in the FA Trophy was annoying, No disrespect to them but it would have been nice to play someone different having gone there only two weeks earlier. This time we had everything going for us. Concord had been narrowly knocked out of the FA Cup four days before in the replay against Mansfield with former Wood player Ollie Palmer scoring the winner. In that time, their star player Jordan Chiedozie had been snapped up by Cambridge United and there was a feeling of "after the Lord Mayor's Show" about the FA Trophy fixture. Again we didn't take into account the fighting spirit of this Concord team. We had Josh Hill ruled out through suspension with recently signed eighteen year old loanee Harry Hickford from MK Dons taking his place alongside Callum Reynolds at the back. Hickford was well thought of at Milton Keynes. When Hickford was younger, his parents, Alan and Sally invited his friend (a fellow youth team player at MK Dons) to live with them to stop him getting into bad habits and mixing with the wrong people. This friend happened to live in a rough part of Milton Keynes in an unstable family environment. His friend went on to live with the Hickford family for the next few years in an environment that would give his undoubted talent a better opportunity to flourish. He finished his education and made his way into the Milton Keynes first team at the age of just sixteen. His name was Dele Alli.

Ian Allinson also decided to start with Angol, Morias, Montgomery and Shakes on the bench with Moli, Lipman, Noto and Scott Thomas stepping in. By half time we were 4-0 down with all the goals being scored from inside the six yard box. It was a disaster. I know Allinson was criticized for resting a number of players but the team we started with should have been good enough to do better. These were players on the fringe of the team who had a point to prove and didn't take their chance. Moli was particularly bad and it was impossible for anyone in the ground not to hear Ian Allinson shouting at him as he was substituted. Fortunately Concord took it easy on us in the second half and the score remained 4-0. Hickford was soon sent back to MK Dons having seemingly and perhaps unfairly taken a lot of the blame for the result. This wasn't the last we saw from him though as he went on to score against Boreham Wood for Chelmsford City on the last day of the regular season while his brother Dele Alli secured a move to Tottenham Hotspur. Hickford was given a two year contract at MK Dons in the summer of 2015 so he can't have been that bad. Boreham Wood were now out on the FA Cup and FA Trophy. Perhaps this was a blessing in disguise as we could now concentrate on the league. My jinx with the FA Trophy since watching Boreham Wood continued.

A few days later we began the defence of the Herts Senior Cup away at Hertford Town. I was looking forward to this as they did the finest catering as any of the grounds I'd ever been too. However I was banished from going as Paula wanted to go to the gym. In her words "it's only the bloody Herts Senior Cup". Fortunately when it came to it, Paula having had a rough day decided she didn't feel like going to the gym after all. She revealed this news to me at 7:25pm. By 7:30pm I was out of the door and probably drove from Boreham Wood to Hertford in record time while salivating over the burger and chips I was about to eat. I arrived about 7:55pm missing the first ten minutes. The match was probably as good as the catering. We had a team made up of reserves and some first teamers and won easily 4-1 with reserve striker Sam Merson looking particularly impressive with two goals.

Returning to league action, we beat Hayes & Yeading 3-0 again on 6th December with two goals from Angol and one from Whichelow. The next fixture a week later was crucial. We had a free Saturday as we had been knocked out of the FA Trophy as had bottom of the table Staines Town. We were due to play them at home on the penultimate Saturday of the season but the fixture was brought forward to 13th December. This worked in our favour as it meant that we would have a vital Saturday off on 18th April. I had pictured us celebrating the League Title that day while we were not playing. To make this fixture change worthwhile, we had to win which we did comfortably 3-0. This was our first victory against Staines in sixteen matches. Making his debut for us that day was Ben

Martin, a centre half signed from St Albans. Ian Allinson felt the need for extra cover at the back and Martin was a good signing with lots of pedigree. He'd won the Conference South two years earlier with Welling United so had the knowhow to help get us out of this league. Although Ben Martin wasn't a roaring success with us, he did okay. However his real contribution was the vast improvement in Josh Hill's performances at the back. With Martin breathing down his neck, this ensured an excellent second half of the season for Josh Hill who didn't want to give up his place in the team without a fight.

The day before the Staines Town match, I had a bit of a brainwave. I don't get many, but this was a good one. As a keen Facebook user, I decided to set up a Facebook group for supporters or anyone remotely interested in Boreham Wood Football Club. There wasn't an online forum for Boreham Wood supporters and I felt that despite our great season and increased attendances home and away, no one was actually talking to each other. There was no debate about performances, players and no talk about Boreham Wood FC in days gone by. Despite our low numbers, a lot of supporters didn't know each other and there was no supporters club. Having never set up a group on Facebook before, this was quite an ordeal. I spent most of that Friday evening trying to do it while trying to decide what to call it. I did the right thing first by asking permission from the club to set the group up. This was granted as long as I put the word "Unofficial" somewhere in the group title. "Wood Army – Boreham Wood FC (Unofficial)" was formed. By the time of the Staines match the following day we already had over a hundred members. The group did help mobilize supporters during the second half of the season and suddenly everyone seemed to know everyone else. The club was now posting news stories on the group as well as on the official club website. Supporters were suddenly reading comments from the group at bedtime instead of doing what they'd normally do at bedtime! Some non-Facebook users joined Facebook just to have access to the group. The group has been a great success and although I started it, the performance of the team and feelgood factor amongst supporters definitely contributed to its success more than I did.

The Saturday after the Staines match, we were away at Eastbourne Borough when I missed my first Boreham Wood match since 4th October at Havant & Waterlooville. Due to pressure from those on the Facebook group, the club put on a minibus for supporters. Unfortunately I had other plans. I had a date with the lovely soul singing legend, PP Arnold at the 100 Club which I didn't want to miss and couldn't be sure I'd be back from Eastbourne in time. Harry was furious as he had to miss the match. To appease him, I took him to White Hart Lane that day to watch Spurs beat Burnley 2-1, a game he enjoyed. However Boreham Wood lost 4-1 at Eastbourne, their first league defeat since 4th October (ironically). This heavy defeat was to be one of several similar performances this season, a great season but in a few matches, we were awful. (Concord away, Basingstoke at home and Whitehawk away spring to mind).

Following the Eastbourne defeat, we would embark upon a busy Christmas period. Two days before Christmas, Boreham Wood fans were treated to some excellent news on the transfer front. The signing of Anthony Jeffrey was announced. "AJ" who had been so brilliant for us the previous season while on loan from Arsenal, returned to the club for the rest of the season. He carried our forward line the season before, prior to the arrival of Angol and Morias. To have these three in our starting line-up was simply frightening. AJ left the club originally to join Wycombe Wanderers but his contract wasn't renewed at the end of the 2013-14 season.

I'm not sure what he'd been doing in the meantime but didn't care. I was convinced this signing would lead us to the league title. Had Jeffery remained at the club, no one would have touched us. We would have won the league at a canter before the end of the season. Unfortunately, it didn't quite happen like that.

By the time of the Boxing Day fixture at home to Bishop's Stortford, our lead had dropped to three points over Bromley who had two games in hand. Stortford were struggling at the wrong end of the table so a straightforward win was expected. However, we had a much harder game then we'd envisaged. Stortford were equally as good as us. The only difference was that we had Lee Angol and they didn't. His two goals gave us a 2-0 victory. By this time Bromley were hot on our heels having won six league games in a row.

It has become a bit of a tradition in the Lewis household to try and go away for a couple of days between Christmas and New Year. The previous year we'd gone to Birmingham. I suggested to Paula that Bath might be quite a good choice this year. It was well known for its Roman history and great scenery. It was also once home of famous novelist Jane Austen. The only other time I'd been there is on a stag do so it was hardly a sightseeing adventure even though I was familiar with plenty of their pubs!! I was generally looking forward to what the area had to offer. Once I'd booked the Premier Inn hotel, I broke the news to Paula that Boreham Wood were actually playing Bath while we were there. What a coincidence!! I did the right thing though, and took the family on an open top bus trip around Bath on the Saturday. Obviously the kids were moaning as we were on an open top bus trip at the end of December!! Let's just say, there was a slight chill in the air. Paula and I enjoyed the splendour of a great city. Bath was obviously a rugby town and the rugby team were playing at home just as we were on the bus trip. I could see the ground from the top deck of the bus and the place was packed. I wondered if "Twerton Park" would be like that the following day. On the Sunday after the second half of the open top bus trip, Harry and I left the ladies shopping and got a taxi from the City Centre to Twerton Park, the world famous home of Bath City Football Club. During the twenty minute taxi ride it became apparent we'd swapped the pleasant City Centre to something not quite so pleasant. The area of Twerton looked grim. I bet the Bath Tourist Board didn't advertise Twerton in any of its brochures!! We arrived at the ground and went straight to the bar to catch the end of the Spurs v Manchester United match before taking our seats in the ground. Twerton Park looked like something from a bygone era, hopelessly out of date and in need of modernization. The match itself was actually the worst part of the weekend. Anthony Jeffery made his second debut for Boreham Wood and proceeded to miss our best chance of a goalless first half. In the first half, we were the better team and should have been in front. It was one of those games where the team who scored first would win it. Unfortunately it was Bath who took the lead after sixty six minutes following a fine goal by Ben Adelsbury. The goal was well deserved as Bath had been the better side since the break. Unfortunately Adelsbury scored a second in the last few minutes to ensure a 2-0 win for the home team. Ultimately Boreham Wood had been poor. Anthony Jeffery wasn't match fit and at this stage Junior Morias was struggling with a hamstring injury that restricted his movement. This limited our usual flow upfront ensuring that this was the first time in twenty three league games this season, we'd failed to get on the scoresheet. Fortunately on the same afternoon Wealdstone did us a favour by holding our nearest rivals Bromley to a 1-1 draw ensuring we had a two point lead at the top going into the New Year albeit having played two games more.

New Year's Day

If Carlsberg did New Year's Days, 1ˢᵗ January 2015 would be high up on its list. It was a day of two fantastic football results and a story of two excellent centre forwards, one of whom just happened to play for Boreham Wood on a one season stop over on his way to better things and the other one of a similar age who was making a name for himself at Spurs.

The day didn't start off well as I had the traditional New Year's Day hangover. We had friends over the previous night and I had a bit too much to drink. Perhaps this was to block out the live performance on TV of the new version of the legendary band Queen. They had a singer called Adam Lambert who had taken over from the great Freddie Mercury and was terrible. Surely Brian May can't be that skint to be involved in something like this!! Unfortunately those I was with were enjoying it so wouldn't switch over. I was convinced my headache in the morning was caused by the sound of Freddie Mercury doing summersaults in his grave!! The fact that this excuse for a band were passing themselves off as Queen was nothing short of scandalous in my opinion. They were a "tribute band". Nothing more, nothing less!! As you have probably gathered, I take my music quite seriously.

We had an early start as kick off was at 1pm in the return match at Bishops Stortford. Fortunately Baz drove and a few of us had a drink in the bar beforehand. Junior Morias was left on the bench as he wasn't fully fit and Allinson played the formation I'd wanted him to play at a number of away games. We had one up front and packed the midfield with the ever dependable Scott Thomas in the starting line-up. I'm not normally a fan of one up front and feel it can only work with a certain type of striker, Drogba at Chelsea for example was a mobile quick forward who is good in the air. Lee Angol fitted that criterion. Everytime he had the ball he'd have two players around him. This meant that the other ten Boreham Wood players only had to worry about another nine. Despite this "tactical masterclass" the match was goalless at half time with very few chances. At half time we moved from the seats to stand behind the goal. There were quite a few away supporters there that day, enough to have a good sing song and the volume rose in the second half. The performance of the players on the pitch may have had something to do with it. As soon as the second half started Stortford player James Walker hit the post when it was easier to score. All of a sudden, a great pass from Cox to Shakes led to him opening the scoring. The away supporters and the bench went wild. A minute later Montgomery came close to adding to his collection of great goals but fired just over. A minute later a wonderful run and cross by Angol led to a second goal for Shakes and Boreham Wood. Angol joined the party five minutes later to make it 3-0. Cox should have added a fourth, missing when it was easier to score. At this point all attention drew towards Cox's father Terry who was stood with us. "Didn't you do shooting practice with him as a kid?", I innocently asked him. We needn't have worried as Whichelow added a fourth following more fantastic work from Angol and Lipman added a fifth, seconds after coming off the bench. We had numerous chances to add more goals and were toying with them in the end. It was embarrassing. Lee Angol was on a different planet that day. It was obvious to anyone who watched him that Angol belonged a number of divisions higher than the Conference South. His career was going nowhere at Wycombe until Ian Allinson saw something in him that no one else could see. The performance from the team in the second half was devastating and convinced me that we were the best team in this division. To make the result even better, Bromley succumbed to a 2-1 defeat at home to Concord Rangers. Even though we'd played two games more we now had a five point lead over Bromley in second place.

Something occurred to a lot of Boreham Wood supporters during and immediately after the Bishops Stortford match. It concerned the whereabouts of Anthony Jeffery. He wasn't in the starting line up or on the bench. We'd assumed he was injured. AJ had performed moderately at Bath City a few days earlier but he wasn't the only one. It turned out that one of our supporters saw him outside the ground before the Stortford game, throwing his football boots in the boot of his car, getting in and driving away. I'm not sure of the exact details but it seems that having been left out of the starting line-up he "threw his toys out of the pram" and walked out. Jeffrey didn't return and left the club that moment only a week after rejoining. This behaviour seemed extremely out of character for a player who did so much for the club in his first spell but the club had done so much for him as well. When he left the club following the end of his loan spell earlier in the year he thanked the club on Twitter for everything they have done for him. He had rejoined a club at the top of the league at an exciting time but it seems it wasn't good enough for him. I assume he had an agent promising him the world. If we had AJ in the team for the rest of the season, we would have easily more than made up the two point gap between us and Bromley and won the league instead of settling for the stress of the play offs.. There were times towards the end of the season that we needed a decent third striker who could come off the bench and score us a goal. The incident didn't do anyone any good, however as it turned out it was worse for the player than for the club. Boreham Wood did go up without AJ and he had to settle for a few matches for Concord Rangers. I'm sure he regretted the incident. He's only young and people make mistakes. Boreham Wood have had a few players on loan from Arsenal over the years. Although they've all seemed to be talented footballers, they lacked the mental toughness needed in the Conference South or perhaps they thought they were too good for this division. With Anthony Jeffery we had something different. He had everything we needed, pace, power, work ethic and goals, I was convinced he'd get better as the season went on. When I look at some of the rubbish Arsene Wenger has played up front, players like Yaya Sanogo, I'd have Jeffery in the side over him any day of the week.

We left Bishop's Stortford in a happy mood and by the end of 1st January 2015 I was even happier. Later on that afternoon Spurs played against eventual Premier League Champions Chelsea at White Hart Lane live on TV. Chelsea were top of the table with only one league defeat all season with Spurs in fifth place. Up to that point Harry Kane had scored fifteen goals that season although most of them seemed to come against poor opposition in the Europa League. There was a thought that he wasn't capable of producing a performance against a decent team. This theory was blown away that day went he scored two fantastic goals in a great performance against Chelsea to help Spurs to a 5-3 win. Victories for Spurs over Chelsea have been quite rare over the last twenty five years and I always savour these results.

There are a lot of similarities between Harry Kane and Lee Angol (apart from the obvious difference in who they played for). Both are of similar age, and came through the youth team at Spurs. Perhaps they played together although my research hasn't found any evidence of this. Both were starting to make a massive impact for their clubs and both cheered me up on New Year's Day 2015. That evening I put the following on Twitter that really summed up my day:

"Lee Angol = Harry Kane – two quite brilliant centre forward displays today"

Four days later we were at home to promotion rivals Ebbsfleet United. The visitors had recently appointed a new manager in Jamie Day. The former Welling United boss was in the middle of a massive spending spree which would dismantle a perfectly good team and replace them with former Football League players who seemed to be looking for a big payday. Had this not happened, I've no doubt they'd have been in the Play Offs at the end of the season. At the time we played them, their core team was still in place with Darryl McMahon, Billy Bricknell and Anthony Cook still at the club. These three players made a massive difference on the day. Despite this Boreham Wood were the better team for most of the game and when Montgomery equalized for Boreham Wood after fifty minutes (following Bricknell's opener) we were the only team that looked like winning. A few minutes later Angol's goal was wrongly ruled out for offside. After seventy five minutes James Russell spilled the impressive McMahon's free kick for Bricknell to put the visitors back in front. This was a cruel blow following an uncharacteristic mistake from Russell. Soon afterwards Cook's cross also found its way into the net to make it 3-1 to Ebbsfleet and the match was over. It was a disappointing defeat after the great performance on New Year's Day.

We've Gotta Get Out of This Place

A week after the disappointing Ebbsfleet defeat we were away at local rivals St Albans City. This was a massive game as not only were we playing our local rivals but our assault on the title had come off the rails to a certain extent in recent weeks having lost three of our last five league games. The St Albans fixture had been eagerly anticipated by our supporters as one hundred and eighty three of us made the short journey to Clarence Park. When I watched the same fixture in 2011 there were about twenty of us. On police advice the fixture was segregated. I parked the car in the car park and we had to walk through the park itself to another entrance to the ground, going through a rickety turnstile, paying £15 to get in which was the most expensive in the division only to be confronted by an appalling poorly maintained terrace with even worse toilet facilities. The catering facilities were a few things on a table rather than the lovely burger van I ate from four years before. Only the home supporters had access to this. Thank god it didn't rain as we were open to the elements. For such a nice area as St Albans to have such a terrible ground is really bad.

As for the teams, St Albans had acquitted themselves really well since promotion and were sitting comfortably in tenth place in the Conference South table. The match itself was fairly uneventful. There was plenty of singing and a few flares going off in the away end. Ricky Shakes gave us the lead early on and after that St Albans played well without really threatening. In the last twenty minutes Boreham Wood had a number of chances to extend their lead. With three minutes left the strike force of Morias and Angol combined brilliantly for Morias to score an unbelievable goal to make it 2-0. The Boreham Wood supporters went berserk as Morias and the team came to celebrate with us. It was one of the best moments in a great season. Harry was right at the front in the middle of the celebrations which he loved. I realised when I got home later that Harry had filmed the goal on his Hudl tablet. The match ended soon afterwards and there was a real mood of celebration among the players and supporters. It was almost as if we were celebrating the League Title itself. I thought about these celebrations as our form dipped over the next few weeks. Perhaps the players and supporters had lost a bit of focus. To be fair, other factors contributed more to the subsequent loss of form. Although we now had an eight point gap at the top of the league, Bromley had four games in hand. This was nowhere near over. In fact I'd have still made Bromley the favourites at that stage especially as this was our last league match for three weeks.

Following the end of the match and the celebration with the players it was time to leave. Despite the fact the St Albans fans had all gone, we had to once again walk through the park to get to the car even though we could see it through the turnstile at the end of the stand. This overzealous stewarding was really beginning to annoy me especially as Linda couldn't walk very far. It was dark as we walked through the park and we noticed our supporters were milling around trying to find a way out. It turned out all the gates were locked!! They hadn't even bothered to leave them open for us. The gate wasn't that high and I could just about get over it. However there were supporters with walking sticks and people who weren't very mobile. A few of us spent the next twenty minutes or so helping supporters over the gate. Young Harry was holding people's bags as we were helping them over. Until this day I didn't really have anything against St Albans City Football Club. I know they were our local rivals but it wasn't the same rivalry as Spurs and Arsenal for instance. My opinion of the club changed from that day. I was so incensed, I wrote the following email to their Chairman Nick Archer on the Monday morning

Mr Chairman

As a Boreham Wood supporter I'd just to write about my disappointment as to the way our supporters were treated on Saturday

The fixture at Boreham Wood earlier in the season was an excellent game of football, a good atmosphere with not an ounce of trouble. In fact there was a lot of good natured banter between the two sets of supporters as far as I'm aware, exactly what a local derby (or any game) should be. St Albans City supporters were treated well with no intimidation and full access to the whole Stadium, burger bars and main bar / clubhouse

1) Despite having someone with us with a walking stick who isn't able to walk very far, we were made to walk around the park to another turnstile when there was a perfectly good turnstile where we parked.

2) We had probably the worst toilet facilities I've ever used at football with no access to any others.

3) I didn't sample it myself but there were lots of complaints about the "makeshift" catering facilities and quality of food on offer, again with no access to anything else. From memory the catering at St Albans City FC had generally been good.

4) At the end of the game Boreham Wood supporters had to leave the ground the way we came in. However all the gates in the park were locked so we all had to climb over a fence to get out!! It wasn't a high fence but bear in mind there were a lot of older people with walking sticks and crutches etc. and it was only the help of other Boreham Wood supporters that ensured everyone got out safely. I appreciate the park being open from the outside has nothing to do with St Albans City FC but I

assume the decision makers at the club know what time the
park is locked or could have requested it stays open longer to let
supporters out. Alternatively the club could have let us out of the
turnstile leading to the car park to avoid the park all together!!
All in all many of us felt that the way Boreham Wood support-
ers were treated on Saturday was outrageous and left many of
our fans wanting some sort of explanation. I would be inter-
ested to know the thought process that went being the events
of Saturday.

I would really appreciate a response and hope to hear from
you soon

Kind Regards
Brett Lewis (Boreham Wood supporter)

I didn't even get a response. There was no apology to Boreham Wood supporters from St Albans City FC. In fact I heard
a rumour that the letter went on the wall in their clubhouse,
no doubt a source of amusement for St Albans officials and
supporters. The whole incident and more importantly the
lack of apology has left me quite bitter towards St Albans City
Football Club.

By the Tuesday night I'd calmed down enough to look
forward to my first ever trip to The Lamex Stadium, home
of Stevenage Football Club for the Herts Senior Cup Quarter
Final tie. It was a fixture that didn't seem to wow the Boreham
Wood public. I gave Baz and Linda a lift in my car but let it
be known that there were two spare spaces. Apart from Phil
Jackson (who would have made his own way there anyway)
no one else wanted a lift. We had about twenty supporters
there that night, three days after having nearly two hundred
fans at St Albans. I wasn't expecting much but what we witnessed that night was something quite sensational. We won

the match 5-3 and I don't remember ever going to a match (Boreham Wood, Spurs, England etc) which had so many fantastic goals. None of it was filmed so those who didn't attend, missed out. Those of us who went, wished we could watch it again.

The home team went in front after nine minutes. Four minutes later Lee Angol won the ball on the halfway time before knocking it over two defenders and running through on goal before chipping the keeper to make it 1-1. A few minutes later Whichelow scored a belter following another great move from Angol. An even better strike from Whichelow followed, this time a cracking volley to make it 3-1 with only twenty minutes on the clock. Stevenage pulled a goal back to make it 3-2 before half time and then equalized after fifty five minutes. The home team was now in the ascendancy until Lee Angol scored a header from a corner a few minutes later to make it 4-3. Not long afterwards Angol was brought down in the penalty area and proved he is human after all by missing the resulting penalty following a good save by keeper Sam Beasant. Beasant's save wasn't quite as famous as his illustrious father Dave Beasant's penalty save for Wimbledon in the 1988 FA Cup Final but it did temporarily deny Lee Angol his hat trick. Angol did eventually complete his hat trick with an unbelievable volley to make it 5-3. If Sam and Dave Beasant were in goal together they'd have never saved that. When Angol was substituted after eighty minutes, even the Stevenage supporters applauded him. I heard him apologise to the Boreham Wood bench for missing the penalty. Luke Garrard responded with "Shut up. You've scored a hat trick".

It was Lee Angol's first ever senior hat trick and one of the best I've ever seen. The match finished 5-3 with Boreham Wood now in the semi-finals. It was a wonderful night that will live long in the memory. What a shame we had to wait nearly three weeks for our next game.

Breaking up is Hard to Do

Unfortunately following the fun and games at St Albans and Stevenage we didn't play again until 31st January. Saturday 17th January was the date scheduled for Salisbury Town and their non-appearance in the league meant we had the Saturday off. The following Saturday we were scheduled to play Farnborough away but they were in the FA Trophy that weekend. This enforced break could have meant either the team was nicely rested in time for the "run in" or, they would lose the momentum from before. Unfortunately the latter occurred.

On 17th January Harry and I went to White Hart Lane again to watch Christian Eriksen score a last minute winner for Spurs against Sunderland 2-1. Towards the end of the match a number of relevant scores started to filter through. Bromley had lost 2-1 to Whitehawk. Ebbsfleet lost at Sutton United and Basingstoke only drew at home to Gosport. Boreham Wood had maintained their eight point gap over Bromley at the top having now played three games more. This was a great day for us even though we weren't playing.

Before the following weekend there was some surprising breaking news from the club. Darryl McMahon had rejoined Boreham Wood on a two and a half year contract from Ebbsfleet. This was a shock as he'd been Ebbsfleet's talisman and best player against us a few weeks earlier. It seems that new Manager Jamie Day wanted to clear the decks and start again at Ebbsfleet. On paper this seemed like a great signing. Macca was well thought of by our Manager and Chairman and had always been a friend to the club during his three years away. Significantly he stayed at Ebbsfleet as Head of their Academy although I'm not sure if a role in the Boreham

Wood PASE scheme was ever an option at this stage. I was happy because we had an older head among young players. I felt he'd be an impact player for the rest of the season and would really come into his own when we got promoted. It was hard to see where Macca would fit into the starting line-up when everything was working so well as it was. I felt, that if we start him, we'd have the build the team around him which wasn't a good idea at this stage of the season.

On Saturday 24th January, Bromley scored a late winner at Basingstoke reducing our lead at the top to five points with them having two games in hand. Fortunately fourth placed Whitehawk lost 3-0 at Concord Rangers.

During this three week break I was approached by a Whitehawk supporter who had just started a Fanzine and wanted to interview a Boreham Wood supporter for its first edition. We were top of the league and had a forthcoming fixture with the Sussex side. I obliged and gave the following interview:

Firstly, what drew you into supporting Boreham Wood? How long have you been following them?

I randomly decided to take my 2 year old daughter to a game in April 2008, Carshalton at home. The match was 0-0 and it was shocking!! However there was something about it that got me hooked. I had missed going to regular football since giving up my Spurs season ticket three years earlier so decided to get season tickets for the next season and have been following them since.

Is Non-League football something you feel passionately about? If so, why?

I do feel passionate about Non-league Football. It's funny but before I started watching Boreham Wood I wasn't the least bit interested in it!! To be honest I'd had enough of the Premier League, the cost of going, how they treat the supporters etc. At non-league level your support is appreciated. You have more affinity with the players and more respect for the time and effort they put in, having to juggle playing football (often in front of small crowds) while holding down a full time job. The motivation they must have is incredible.

As we all know Boreham Wood are having an exceptional season; what are the main reasons - both long-term and short term - for the success?

Yes, it has been an exceptional season so far. There is a long way to go. There are many reasons for this both long and short term.

Long Term – *A stable well run club with the same Chairman for 15 years and the same First Team Manager for 6 years. In that time the club has built up a number of revenue streams not related to the fortunes of the First Team. These including a successful Academy – PASE Scheme (Programme for Academic and Sporting Excellence), artificial pitch hire and impressive Banqueting facilities as well as Arsenal Ladies and Development Squad using our ground for home games. This income has no doubt added to the First Team budget. Revenue from our attendances at home games alone wouldn't be nearly enough to sustain a club like ours at Conference South level without someone throwing loads of money at it!!*

Short Term – *A stable team with many players having been with the club a while. Most of last season was disappointing though. However we showed vast improvement during the second half of the season aided by a couple of centre forwards on loan who scored plenty of goals. Last summer was key in that we managed to keep all the players we wanted from last season including the strikers, while adding a few in key areas and have managed to score 56 league goals (at the time of writing) so far which is far more than anyone else in the league.*

Down at Whitehawk we regularly on our travels get vilified and shouted at by often larger and more established teams such as Eastbourne, Wealdstone and Farnborough. They don't like smaller teams are doing exceptionally well. Is this something you have experienced at the Wood?

I know Whitehawk is where it all started for "The Wealdstone Raider". We also get vilified as well for having "no fans". They don't like smaller teams doing well especially if their club isn't doing well. People wonder how we're doing so well on our at-

tendances and lots of people assume that Arsenal are funding us or we have a philanthropist with deep pockets throwing money at the club. Neither is true.

I have heard much of the 'Wood Army'. How would you characterize the Boreham Wood fan base?

We have a number of loyal supporters that go home and away as well as a few who just come to home games. The problem is, the fan base is small and wouldn't look out of place 2 divisions further down. Like most clubs at our level, we're surrounded by bigger clubs which include the likes of Spurs, Arsenal, Watford and even Barnet. It annoys me a bit that certain supporters only bother turning up when there is a big cup game. I suppose it happens everywhere. Borehamwood as an area doesn't seem to have that community spirit that other places have. Perhaps this is reflected its support for its local club. Hopefully continued success will add to our fan base.

Your youth academy is fantastic. Do you have any young talent who you think can really make it up to league-football?

The youth academy is fantastic, offering a great opportunity to young footballers. Bear in mind I only go to first team matches it's hard for me to pinpoint any particular current players. However the PASE Scheme has produced a number of league players in the past playing at clubs such as Watford, Luton and West Ham as well as across the non-league pyramid. It has also produced a number of College England internationals.

Are you making the trip down to Brighton to watch Boreham Wood at the Hawks? Have you seen much of Whitehawk and do you think you can get a result?

I'm confident of getting a result but sadly Whitehawk away is one game I'm gonna have to miss this season as I'm on holiday at the time. I went to watch Boreham Wood there last year though in the wettest, windiest game I've been to!! Fortunately we won 2-0. You did however beat us at our place. It's clear that your team has vastly improved since last season. The first season in the Conference South is always hard. Some of your players are familiar including Osei Sankofa, a good player for Boreham Wood a few years ago as well as Sergio Torres, ex Crawley.

Finally, and a one word answer will do, this time next year will Boreham Wood be a Conference Premier side?

I've got to be confident. YES!! Maybe Whitehawk will join us!!

Following the start and finish of my brief career as a journalist we finally had a match to play. On 31st January Boreham Wood hosted play-off contenders Basingstoke Town at Meadow Park in our first league match in three weeks. McMahon surprisingly came straight into the starting line-up replacing Montgomery on the left. The match started promisingly with us having the better of the first twenty minutes until Basingstoke took the lead with Chris Flood scoring the first of his three goals. The eventual 4-0 defeat was well deserved as Basingstoke were all over us. To make matters worse Bromley beat Havant & Waterlooville to reduce our gap at the top of the league to two points and we'd played two games more.

Before the Basingstoke match it was announced there would be a club minibus to take supporters to Whitehawk the following Saturday. Unfortunately I missed the trip to Sussex as I went to Antwerp for my friend Darren's stag do. Linda very kindly offered to take Harry to (or look after him on the minibus) and he really wanted to go. However Paula wasn't keen on him going so far without me. We promised him that he could go to the Havant & Waterlooville match on 28th February at home without me. It was the day of Darren's wedding.

The week before the Whitehawk match, Austin Lipman returned to Arsenal as his appearances were limited. It was a shame because he could have been a good impact player for the rest of the season. Lewis Toomey left the club for Kings Langley as he also failed to make an impression.

While the rest of the "Wood Army" were on the minibus to Whitehawk I was having a fantastic time sampling the delights of Antwerp and the various museums and art galleries!! On the Saturday morning a few of us went to a great Irish bar to watch the Spurs Vs Arsenal match on TV. This was a massive game as at the time the two teams were neck and neck in the league. I enjoyed a massive breakfast and a few pints but wasn't enjoying the first half because despite Spurs playing well, Arsenal went into the break 1-0 up. It all changed in the second half when Harry Kane equalized. I went absolutely potty and shouted a number of swear words in celebration just as a five foot tall Belgium barmaid, scared out of her mind, started collecting our empty glasses. The poor woman had the fright of her life. I did the right thing and apologized. When Kane scored the winner with five minutes left I went potty again. It's always good when Spurs beat Arsenal. From my understanding the mostly Arsenal supporting "Wood Army" gathered in the Whitehawk clubhouse to watch the match. As I sat in the Irish bar for the rest of the afternoon, my attention was drawn to the Whitehawk match. Sadly BT Sport weren't showing the match so I had to rely on Boreham Wood supporters to drip feed information to the Facebook group. Unfortunately the news given to me from East Brighton wasn't good. Boreham Wood lost 3-0 and by all accounts it was an even worse performance than against Basingstoke. McMahon was picked in central midfield when surely Scott Thomas would have been a better bet there. To compound a dreadful day for Boreham Wood, Bromley hammered bottom club Staines Town 6-0 and went top by one point with two games in hand. The chasing pack of Whitehawk, Havant and Basingstoke were closing in. Our season looked like imploding.

You Can Get It If You Really Want

Fortunately we had a match on the Monday night, the rearranged game at Farnborough. Sometimes after two morale sapping defeats, it's good to get another game out of the way as soon as possible, especially against a team as out of form as Farnborough were. I was safely back in the UK and although I felt rather jaded following all those museums and art galleries, I made the trip to Hampshire for the match. The starting line-up that night at Farnborough faced some harsh facts! Out of the starting line-up went McMahon, left back Jordan Browne, Ben Martin and Graeme Montgomery. Browne had played his last match for the club and was released soon afterwards. In came Scott Thomas, Josh Hill, Junior Morias and new loanee Tyrell Miller-Rodney making his debut. Sam Cox filled in at right back with Luke Garrard moving to left back. Morias was in a slightly withdrawn role with Angol up front on his own. Farnborough were second from bottom and had lost their last five league matches. Surely this was a great time for us to get back on track. Not a lot happened in the first half. The match was being played by two teams lacking in confidence. Our team had an imbalance to it that night and we were crying out for some width down the left hand side. Fortunately after sixty one minutes Montgomery came on to replace Miller-Rodney with Morias taking his usual position alongside Angol upfront. Suddenly the whole dynamics of the match changed and our confidence came flooding back. After sixty nine minutes Montgomery opened the scoring with an excellent volley. A cracking run and shot from Morias added a second a few minutes later and then, it was a question of how many we were going to get. During the rest of the match I was arguing with a number of Farnborough supporters who were slagging off Lee Angol for diving even though he was being fouled constantly by the Farnborough defenders. I remember shouting "he's the best player you'll ever see at this shit club". Angol shut them up by adding the third from the penalty spot in injury time which was no less than his excellent performance deserved. It was his twentieth league goal of the season. Lee Angol's mother, sitting close by came up to me at the end and thanked me for defending her son. Josh Hill had returned to the starting line up in style that night and wasn't going to give up his place to Ben Martin again. Hill thrived on the pressure put on him by having Martin waiting in the wings. In my opinion he was the best player we had from the Farnborough match onwards. Boreham Wood returned to the top of the league that night as no other Conference South matches took place. Farnborough were a poorly run club who always seemed to be in financial trouble. They got relegated at the end of the season.

Over the next couple of weeks some significant changes were made to the squad. Daryl McMahon was supposed to be the experienced signing that would get us over the line. That honour actually fell to 29 year old full back Ben Herd who we signed from Dunstable, initially to play right back prior to Ben Nunn's return and eventually as left back for the rest of the campaign. Herd had a good pedigree. He had started off in the Watford youth team and he went on to play for Shrewsbury and Aldershot. Notable former teammates of his were Joe Hart and Ashley Young. Herd fitted in straight away like he'd been playing for Boreham Wood for ages. What a difference it would have made to our final league placing if we'd signed Herd earlier in the campaign. Centre forward Charlie Walker arrived on loan from Luton Town until the end of the season to add some much needed backup to Angol and Morias. Walker had joined Luton Town in the summer of 2014 from Ryman League South side Peacehaven & Telscombe when he'd scored over forty goals the previous season. He hadn't broken into the team at Luton so joined us. The form of Angol and Morias meant Walker was a bit part player for us who often came off the bench to hold the ball up and protect our lead. He did this rather well. Ben Nunn finally arrived back from his travels in mid-February and was soon ready to resume first team duties. He looked a lot fitter and leaner then I would have been after six months of living it up in Australia.

The Saturday after the Farnborough match we were at home to Concord Rangers. Ben Herd made his debut and was the best player on the pitch. Unfortunately we had to settle for a 0-0 draw. The following Saturday we made the long trip to Weston Super Mare on the minibus. The Weston match was thoroughly entertaining with McMahon having his best game in either spell at the club. He should have scored in the first minute but made up for it after thirty three minutes with an exquisite cross for Lee Angol to head home to make it 1-0. Wood doubled their advantage after fifty nine minutes through Ricky Shakes. McMahon made it 3-0 a few minutes later via a wicked deflection. Substitute Charlie Walker marked his debut with a goal on eighty nine minutes before a Weston consolation goal made it 4-1. We maintained our two point advantage over Bromley although they had three games in hand.

Saturday 28th February was quite a significant day. Not only did Boreham Wood have a must win home match against fourth placed Havant & Waterlooville but it was the first time Harry went to a match without me. I had my friend Darren's wedding at The Grimsdyke Hotel. Although this was close enough, I doubted the groom would have been pleased if I left his festivities for a football match. As well as that I had to think about all the food and drink I would have missed out on!! Linda very kindly picked Harry up and dropped him home afterwards where my mum was looking after him and Sara. By the time the match started at 3pm I was well underway with the drink, sinking pints like they were going out of fashion. I followed the match on Twitter and was delighted that Lee Angol put us in front in the first minute. Havant equalized with a penalty after forty minutes and the half time score remained 1-1. Early in the second half, Ben Nunn came back on a football field for the first time since September and was quickly sent off for a "professional foul" which resulted in a Havant penalty. Fortunately, this time the penalty was missed. I was following proceedings closely. Boreham Wood and Bromley both drawing but in the last minute it felt like my world had caved in. Bromley scored a last minute winner at Chelmsford while Havant did likewise against us. Our 2-1 defeat was gut wrenching especially with Bromley winning. At this point I had a quick look at the league table and was convinced we'd blown it, not just the league but a play-off spot altogether. As I was sitting on a step outside the toilets with my head in my hands, a woman I didn't know asked me if I was okay. I lied and said I just had a bit of a headache. How do you explain to someone you don't know that your team's season is imploding before your eyes and there isn't a damn thing you could do about it? Bromley had three games in hand and were now one point ahead of us. The league was as good as over. Fifth placed Havant were only four points behind us with one game in hand. I recovered from the blow to enjoy the rest of the evening (it's amazing what loads of red wine can do) but the poor result was always in the back of my mind. Young Harry enjoyed going to football without me. The way we were now playing, I was considering making it a regular thing!

The following Tuesday night, Bromley as good as wrapped up the title in my mind, with a 2-1 win at Sutton and were now leading by four points with two games in hand. Basingstoke having also won, were only two points behind us in third place with a game in hand. Maidenhead United away on

Saturday 7th March was massive. On that day, results around us could hardly have gone any better. Bromley lost at home to Ebbsfleet. Basingstoke only drew at Chelmsford and Havant & Waterlooville lost at Weston Super Mare. The Maidenhead match was tricky. Although we had the better of the first half, the home team was better after the break. We worked hard to stay in the match with a masterclass performance from Scott Thomas in midfield. Thomas had been in and out of the team all season but as the season wore on, he became a vitally important player in front of the back four. In the eighty-second minute, Morias ran in on goal and following an excellent save from the Maidenhead keeper, Ricky Shakes scored from the rebound to give us a massive three points. The "Wood Army" now larger in numbers, went berserk. I'd all but given up a week ago but now we were in pole position for the play offs and with an outside chance again of overtaking Bromley at the top. Bromley were now only one point ahead with two games in hand. My gloom from the week before had lifted. I firmly believe that Shakes' goal that day was pivotal to our season. Had we failed to capitalize on those around us slipping up that day, I believe the outcome to our season could have very different. The Maidenhead match could have been significant for other reasons. Lee Angol collected his ninth booking of the season late on and was one booking away from a two match ban. This would hang over him until 11th April when it would be wiped clean. While Angol somehow avoided that booking, we perhaps didn't see the best of him during that period. Maybe the booking was on his mind. Perhaps it was just coincidence.

On the Tuesday following the Maidenhead match, we secured our second successive trip to the Herts Senior Cup Final, following a straightforward 2-0 win against St Albans at Meadow Park. The following Saturday we were at home to fourth place Whitehawk. Baz, Linda, Harry and I swapped our usual seats to stand behind the goal for this game. We hadn't won at home since Boxing Day and it was no coincidence that the atmosphere was better at away matches. We were determined to lend our voices to the cause even though our view of the match was more restricted. Linda's folding chair became a feature in the Boreham Wood end both home and away for the rest of the season. We were fantastic in the first half and should have been more than a Junior Morias goal in front. Whitehawk predictably came back at us in the second half and scored twice in a ten minute spell to go 2-1 in front. Fortunately Shakes was on hand to equalise with ten minutes left and the score remained 2-2. We should have won but could have lost. Another late Shakes goal got us out of trouble.

Broken Stones

The following weekend we were away at Wealdstone who were holding their own in mid-table following promotion from the Ryman League the previous season. Wealdstone FC was very much on the map at this time because of one individual who just happened to be in the right place at the right time. The "Wealdstone Raider" was one of the most recognizable characters in Britain at the time and even had a song at Number Five in the UK Chart. It all started for Gordon Hill two years earlier during a Ryman League match when Wealdstone played at Whitehawk. He was filmed having what can only be described as an altercation with a Whitehawk fan (or fans) when he explained that they were shit and had "no fans". This clip was put on YouTube. It took a while to catch on but by the later part of 2014, it spread like wildfire making Gordon Hill a star. The name "Wealdstone Raider" was adopted and it stuck. When I first saw the clip,

I recognised "The Wealdstone Raider" straight away. I didn't know him personally but he used to drink in The Whittington pub in Pinner which I used to frequent years ago. Everywhere Wealdstone FC played, he would be mobbed. The week after our match, Wealdstone were away at Basingstoke and apparently it was like One Direction being surrounded by a load of teenage girls!! A Wealdstone supporting friend of mine was there and he said it was quite funny. Gordon Hill didn't seek this fame and from my understanding didn't feel comfortable with it. I saw a documentary about him on You-Tube where he said he wished he had never bothered going to that Whitehawk match in the first place!!

I have always enjoyed going to Ruislip Social Club, the bar at Wealdstone FC. It's a massive set up with a few different rooms and a nice old fashioned bar. I've been there for a couple of Ska gigs in the past. We got there early and the locals were very friendly. I recognised a couple of old faces from Pinner and it was good to catch up with them. I saw The "Wealdstone Raider" at the bar and he was being left alone. I can imagine it was one of the only places he felt normal.

As we sat down, I noticed a flyer for "The Rolling Kitchen". This was a "ground breaking initiative, which will see the club not only transform its on-site catering but partner with two Michelin star trained chef". The prices were a bit steep but it's what you expect to pay for that quality. I was keen to seize the opportunity for some of this "posh grub" so Harry and I walked round to the "Rolling Kitchen" van in the freezing cold. I bought a burger for me and some chips for him. When we returned to the bar, I started munching on the burger. It didn't taste right but I stupidly continued to eat it. I could have taken it back but it was a long walk and being a greedy sod, I decided to finish it. I regretted this decision almost immediately and a number of times during the match and over the next couple of days! On the Monday I emailed the chap from the "Rolling Kitchen" explaining what happened and that something may have been wrong with the burger. While I wasn't expecting him to admit liability, I did at least expect a response. By the Wednesday I didn't get a reply so I mentioned my experience on the Conference South Fans Forum. I was more annoyed with the lack of response then the fact that the food didn't agree with me. Soon afterwards the chap from the "Rolling Kitchen" slagged me off on the Wealdstone Fans Forum saying that I was trying to ruin his business. I assume he hadn't expected me to read it. At that point he still hadn't come back to me directly. By the Thursday he did respond to me saying it couldn't possibly be his food as "his goods are made of the finest ingredients". I suggested that if he'd put his nose in "Trap 2" of the men's toilets a number of times during the match, he'd have got all the evidence he needed!! It all got a bit nasty with some of the emails going back and forward. In the end we agreed to disagree and I let it go. Had he responded to me directly, I wouldn't have even mentioned it in this book. I certainly wouldn't have gone on the Conference South Forum to criticise them.

Back to the Wealdstone match, the turnout of Boreham Wood supporters was poor that day. Bear in mind it was such an important match and a local derby of sorts, we only had about thirty supporters there. However, didn't we make some noise though? The match itself was fairly uneventful and with Wealdstone producing very little, I had a feeling that one goal would be enough. This goal duly arrived in injury time at the end of the first half courtesy of a Ricky Shakes header. This fellow was unstoppable. It was one of a number of vital goals he'd scored in recent weeks. Whatever he was paid during his six months out injured at the start of his time at the club, he'd more than earnt since returning to the team.

During the second half, Boreham Wood worked like dogs to keep the lead but couldn't add to their one goal lead. The "Wood Army" erupted half way through the second half with the news that rock bottom Staines Town had taken the lead at top of the table Bromley. As we were talking about it, the Wealdstone goalkeeper Jonathan Bond turned to us in utter amazement and said "Staines are beating Bromley?" as if he couldn't quite believe it. We managed to hold out for a 1-0 win. Staines secured a similar score at Bromley, helped by the home team missing a last minute penalty. Bromley were now only one point ahead of us with a game in hand. We were back in the title race. The match we had at Bromley two weeks later would be crucial. Three weeks before I had my head in my hands at a wedding thinking that we'd blown it. Now I was dreaming again!!

I'm Only Dreaming

With only five games left, we were now very well placed going into the Hemel Hempstead game on 28th March. The way Bromley seemed to be imploding, I was convinced we could go there on Easter Saturday and win. If we did, I felt the title would be ours. The Boreham Wood team has taken on a different feel to earlier in the season. At that time we would often win with free flowing football and would rely on individual brilliance from players like Angol and Montgomery. This inevitably led to some heavy defeats too. Following the heavy defeats against Basingstoke and Whitehawk things had to change. Perhaps we'd been found out. Ricky Shakes moved from central midfield to right midfield and Scott Thomas replaced him in the middle. This gave our back four more protection. This worked a treat for the remainder of the season but it meant that we'd often be hanging on for a win not doing my blood pressure any good!!.

The Hemel Hempstead match, the week after the Weald-stone win was an example of this. Hemel were having an excellent season following promotion the year before so this wasn't going to be easy, especially as we hadn't won at home since Boxing Day. An excellent crowd of nearly six hundred supporters saw a nail biting match won for Boreham Wood by an excellent low shot from Morias after twenty six minutes. Our attention was drawn towards Bromley's match at mid table Bath City. After thirty five minutes Bromley had raced into a 2-0 lead so we all assumed that was over. Bath had nothing to play for and Bromley were in pole position for the title. As our game became more and more tense, I'd forgotten about events elsewhere and even news of a Bath goal to make it 2-1 after fifty-nine minutes didn't really register with me. The collective sigh of relief at our 1-0 win was there for all to see. At that point I got a call from a friend of mine to say that Bath has equalized in the last minute and the final score was 2-2. He wasn't even a Boreham Wood fan but I noted the excitement in his voice. Word spread about news of Bath's late equaliser. While the players were still on the pitch a chorus of "we are top of the league" spread amongst the Boreham Wood supporters. We were now back on top of the league by one point having played one game more. A "Wealdstone Raider" inspired Wealdstone did us a massive favour by winning impressively at Basingstoke. This opened up a five point gap between us in second place and them in third. We knew a second placed finish would give Boreham Wood home advantage should we get to the Play-Off Final. However a win at Bromley the following Saturday would give us the upper hand in the race for the title. I actually felt a draw might be good enough to give us the initiative too. The atmosphere in the bar after the Hemel match was electric.

There was a lot of singing among supporters and a genuine belief that we could snatch the title off Bromley.

The week of the Bromley match was very tense. That tension extended to the Lewis household. The Friday and Saturday were the first two days of the Jewish festival "Passover" and Paula felt that I shouldn't go to the Bromley match. Harry and I convinced her that the match wasn't a matter of life or death but more important than that!! I arranged to meet my brother Elliot and nephew Finn at the match. As well as that I had a long standing arrangement to meet a couple of my old friends Nick and Ian who wanted to come to the game. I used to go to Spurs with them in the early 1990's and had recently got back in touch with them via Facebook. Spurs weren't playing and they were keen to sample a Boreham Wood match probably because they'd heard me bang on about them! The fact that it was a top of the table clash made the fixture more appealing to them.

On the day of reckoning, Saturday 4th April we met up early at the club to board the minibus as a number of our supporters wanted to watch the Arsenal v Liverpool match on television in the bar at Bromley Football Club which kicked off at 12:45pm. This suited me because it meant I had more time to have a catch up with my brother Elliot, as well as Nick and Ian. Just before we left Boreham Wood a few of us had a couple of words with Assistant Manager Luke Garrard who was extremely confident ahead of the game. We also had a chance to congratulate him as he'd just become a father for the first time a few days before. At this time I was imagining players and supporters sitting in the bar two weeks later when we didn't have a game, hearing other results come in that would confirm us as champions. We had this rather important match to negotiate first. The journey to Bromley was fairly quick and we got in the bar at about

12:30pm. We met up with my brother, nephew and my two friends and had a good catch up while drinking a number of pints of some Japanese lager. When the match got under way it was quite even for the first few minutes. However after fourteen minutes a McMahon corner was headed in by Josh Hill to give Boreham Wood a 1-0 lead followed by mass celebrations from the travelling supporters. We had taken an early lead and were more than capable of either adding to the lead or holding on to see the game out. Bromley then had more of the ball but I always felt that we had another goal in us. We were holding out comfortably. However on the hour mark Bromley wide man Anthony Cook took a tumble in the penalty box and the referee pointed to the spot. Even from the other end of the pitch this looked harsh. Cook made no mistake from the spot to equalise and the score was now 1-1. With ten minutes left on the clock Bradley Goldberg scored what turned out to be the winner for Bromley when our defence was caught napping. The 2-1 defeat was heartbreaking especially as we'd looked comfortable for most of the match. Bromley had almost sown up the title as they were now two points ahead with a game in hand. However Boreham Wood only had three matches left. If we won them all, we had to rely on Bromley only winning two of their remaining four matches to have a chance. Although I felt this was nigh on impossible, Bromley had shown signs of imploding in recent weeks so who knows. Following the match we were standing around outside the club when we spoke to an angry Ian Allinson who was moaning about the referee and the penalty decision that went against us. We also spoke at length to the Bromley Manager Mark Goldberg. He was very friendly as he'd always been when I'd spoken to him in the past. Mark Goldberg is famous because having made a fortune in recruitment he bought Crystal Palace Football Club in 1998 and lost everything in the process. Somehow he ended up in football management and was in his third spell as manager of Bromley Football Club. Amazingly, the Bromley defeat meant we'd failed to beat any of our eventual play off rivals in the league home or away. The journey back from Bromley was fairly eventful with some of our supporters demanding a toilet stop almost as soon as we got on the M25. This was fairly amusing to me as I'd always made a point of not drinking too much when I'm about to board a vehicle without a toilet. It's a shame others didn't have this self-control. I always feel the joy of having a few extra pints isn't worth the pain of needing the toilet. The eventual toilet stop just off the M25 near London Colney was greeted with relief and triumph by some of those on board. Harry shared this relief and triumph. My request to stop at the Arsenal Training Ground (a few hundred yards up the road) to "go about our business" was rudely rejected by an Arsenal supporter dominated minibus!! There was a funny photograph taken of loads of us lining up against a bush doing what we needed to do. With the rest of my family out I treated young Harry to DVD and a fish and chips take-away, comfort eating after a disappointing day.

We only had two days to wait for our next match which was at home to Sutton on Easter Monday. The events of the Monday convinced me that despite the shattering defeat on Saturday at Bromley, the league was far from over. The match against Sutton was like so many in recent weeks. It was a hard fought encounter where the Sutton side gave as good as they got. Callum Reynolds scored a rare goal to give us the lead after sixteen minutes and news filtered through that Bromley were 2-0 down at Maidenhead, again the Kent side seemed determined to throw their advantage away. We stayed 1-0 up until the sixty sixth minute when Lee Angol scored his first goal in five matches with a brilliant free kick to settle our nerves. This was the first evidence that this rather special player had a free kick like that in his locker. He would show it again twice more in the next few weeks. As our match ended, Bromley were 4-3 up at Maidenhead and our hopes were almost gone. However we had some *déjà vu* and as the players were applauding the fans at Meadow Park, news came through of a late equalizer for Maidenhead to make the final score 4-4 in what must have been a crazy game at York Road. We were now top on goal difference although we'd played one match more than Bromley. Another chorus of "we are top of the league" occurred among the Wood supporters. The players looked at each other in amazement. I felt that if we could win both our remaining matches the title was still a possibility but Bromley had to lose one of their final three games. Bromley had two straight forward looking matches at home against Eastbourne Borough and Weston Super Mare followed by a tricky away match at Gosport Borough. We also had to watch Basingstoke who were hot on our heels in third place two points behind but with a game in hand. I'd given up trying to predict any scores at this stage of such a bizarre season.

On Saturday 11th April we had a tricky away match at Ebbsfleet United while Bromley hosted Eastbourne and Basingstoke had a hard match at Sutton United. Ebbsfleet had blown hot and cold since we played them in January and their unnecessary squad overhaul played a big part in it. Dr Abdulla Al-Humaidi, the Kuwaiti owner of Ebbsfleet United FC declared as early as March that they wouldn't get promoted this season and were gearing themselves for a title challenge in the 2015-16 season. It surprised me that he was throwing in the towel so early. We arrived at Ebbsfleet early and entered the ground as soon as it opened. Before going into the bar, we stood by the pitch speaking to a few of the players who were about to warm up. We noticed Daryl McMahon (who was injured) talking to a few Ebbsfleet players. It was as if he'd never actually left. In truth he hadn't as Macca was still Academy Manager there. While I didn't think anything untoward, I thought about this following what happened ten days later. More about that soon. We headed to the bar and had what had become a traditional pre match drink with other Boreham Wood supporters, a few of whom carried on a massive drinking session in a bar at St Pancras Station on their way home. Apparently one or two of them didn't remember getting home!!

The match was very eventful and tense. Ebbsfleet were exceptional, especially in the first half. They took a well-deserved lead just before half time and looked like adding a second. Later in the match Ian Allinson replaced Angol (who was carrying a knock) with Charlie Walker, Montgomery with Whichelow and Ricky Shakes with Ben Martin. Martin would play as part of a back three with full backs Nunn and Herd pushed further forward. At this point, we started to turn up the pressure. With three minutes left, an excellent pass by Sam Cox found Walker in the penalty area who was fouled as he was about to shoot. Barry and I were appealing for a penalty like a couple of demented fast bowlers on "crack"! I thought the referee wasn't going to give it. It seemed like an eternity until he finally pointed to the spot. With our regular penalty taker, Lee Angol off the pitch, Ben Nunn stepped up. He scored from the spot at the Herts Senior Cup Final the previous season so I had every confidence he would put it away. Nunn proceeded to bury it in the top corner to make it 1-1. No goalkeeper in the world would have saved that. The Wood Army went into raptures. Unfortunately Bromley won 2-1 so we needed another goal to have a chance of the title. With the last kick of the game Charlie Walker fired over the bar following a good move. Standing behind the goal, Harry caught the ball and the referee blew the whistle with the final score 1-1. Our heads were in our hands. It was a great effort to get back into the game when it looked lost. Bromley now only needed one win in their final two matches to clinch the title. Some good news came out of Gander Green Lane, home of Sutton United, as the home team scored a last minute winner to beat Basingstoke. We were now three points ahead of Basingstoke having played a game more. This meant that with our superior goal difference, a win at Chelmsford on the last day of the season would ensure second place and home advantage should we get to a Play Off Final. Having played Staines Town earlier in the season, we now had two weeks until our next league match. This break was perfect as it gave Lee Angol time to get over a niggling injury before the play offs.

On the Tuesday night we had the Herts Senior Cup Final against Hemel Hempstead at the appalling County Ground, Letchworth. We had near enough a full strength side out but Angol was rested with Charlie Walker playing instead. The pitch was dreadful and the Boreham Wood side played like they had other things on their minds. The year before, the Herts Senior Cup Final meant a bit more but this time there was a far greater prize on offer. The match was poor and it was obvious that one goal would win it. The goal came from a great Jordan Parkes free kick for Hemel on the hour mark. Hemel ran out 1-0 winners and the players and supporters of Boreham Wood didn't seem to care too much.

With a spare Saturday coming up, I intended to keep a long standing promise to Paula to clear the garage out and take the contents to the dump and the charity shop. These plans were changed at twenty four hours' notice by what turned out to be a masterstroke by Boreham Wood Chairman Danny Hunter. The Chairman, perhaps sensing a bit of nervousness in the camp, announced that a Question & Answer afternoon would take place at the club on the Saturday afternoon. It would occur after the first team training session and before the reserves were due to play a cup semi-final on the AstroTurf pitch. To entice a few greedy people like me, there was some food laid on. Never being one to pass up the opportunity of free grub, Sara joined me and Harry for the afternoon. (I wonder where she gets it from). The speech by the Chairman to players and supporters was similar to that of Al Pacino's in "Any Given Sunday". It was inspirational. I turned up for the afternoon a little nervous about what would happen over the next few weeks and came away absolutely convinced we would go up. I've no doubt this rubbed off on the players and other supporters too. There was a mood of togetherness among the supporters, staff and players. The management team of Ian Allinson, Luke Garrard, Mario Noto and the Chairman as well as Callum Reynolds and Sam Cox sat on stage with a number of questions going back and forward. During the afternoon it was nice to speak to the players and other supporters in a relaxed environment. The scores from other games started to filter through. Bromley secured the title with a 3-0 win over Weston Super Mare and no one seemed to care. There was no "head in hand" or disappointment in the bar. Bromley only confirmed what we already knew. Often when a team misses out on the title, it might be a final day heartache where it's difficult to then lift themselves for the play offs. Significantly this wasn't a factor for us this season. More significantly perhaps was that Basingstoke only managed to draw 0-0 with Havant & Waterlooville (who'd also secured a play-off spot) meaning that Boreham Wood only needed a draw at Chelmsford on the final day of the season to secure second place and home advantage in a play-off final should we get there. Whitehawk confirmed their place in the play offs with a 3-1 victory over Hemel Hempstead. Later on in the afternoon we ventured out to the Astroturf pitches to watch the reserves play. Charlie Hunter scored the winner from a free kick from the half way line!! It was probably the only time a match on the AstroTurf has ever been accompanied by a chant of "Wood Army" by a watching crowd. The feelgood factor was definitely on show that day at Boreham Wood. The following day I kept my promise to Paula by clearing the garage out and making four visits to the dump and three to the charity shop.

The week before the Chelmsford match was very interesting. It started on the Monday with the surprising news that Jamie Day had been sacked as Ebbsfleet United manager after only four months in charge. I immediately thought they'd try to get Daryl McMahon to take over and mentioned this during a debate on the Facebook group that day. Macca had been Caretaker Manager earlier in the season when previous manager Steve Brown was dismissed. I knew he'd signed a long term contract for us only a few months earlier but if offered the role at Ebbsfleet United, I had no doubt he'd take it. Some assumed that with Ebbsfleet's expensively assembled squad, they may want a more experienced manager to look after all the egos! As far as I was concerned, with McMahon already a part of the fabric of the club, he was the obvious choice. By the Wednesday the announcement was made that McMahon was indeed going to take over at Ebbsfleet with immediate effect and I was saying "I told you so" to a lot of people. I wasn't too worried about the sudden departure as I didn't think we'd miss him as a player. Being superstitious, I was acutely aware that Daryl McMahon was something of a jinx in play-off finals having lost in his last four!!

Saturday 25ᵗʰ April was the final day of the regular season and we were away at Chelmsford where we only needed to avoid defeat to secure second place. I was feeling ill by this stage and had a horrible hacking cough that would carry on for weeks. The match itself was an absolute cracker. Lee Angol gave us the lead with another brilliant free kick after fifteen minutes only for Chelmsford to equalise soon afterwards. Goals from Reynolds and Morias gave us a 3-1 lead just after half time. However two goals for Chelmsford midway through the second half made it 3-3. With Basingstoke winning 2-1 at Weston Super Mare, we had to hold out and not lose. Fortunately with nine minutes on the clock, Montgomery scored the winner to make it 4-3 following an excellent team move. Following this result we finished two points behind Bromley and two points ahead of Basingstoke in third place. We fully expected to be playing Whitehawk away in the first leg of the Play off Semi Final on the Wednesday night. They were away at Havant & Waterlooville in their final league fixture. Whitehawk had to win this match to avoid us which they did with a late winner, securing a 2-1 victory. We were delighted to avoid Whitehawk as we felt they presented a bigger challenge than Havant & Waterlooville. If we were to eventually meet them, it would be in the final at home, in front of our supporters.

That night we had our End of Season Presentation Night at the Holiday Inn. Some might say, it was a bit premature bearing in mind we still had the play offs. However these events are usually planned well in advance. I wasn't sure what the evening would be like because the players still had so much to do. I needn't have worried as the feelgood factor generated by the question & answer afternoon continued. It was probably the most enjoyable end of season do since the one that followed the 2010 Ryman League Play Off Final. The players and supporters were eating drinking and dancing together. There were motivational speeches by the Chairman and Club President Bill O'Neill. If these speeches didn't inspire the players, they certainly inspired me. It was great to see loyal supporter Phil Jackson win the Supporter of the Year award. Phil didn't just jump on the bandwagon because we were successful. He was following Boreham Wood FC when things weren't so good and he'd often be one of only a handful of supporters at away games having undertaken all kinds of public transport to get there. If any supporter deserved to see the success the club was now having, it was him. Phil has an incredible memory of matches he's watched over the years including results, scorers and attendances etc. If this book was a "facts and figures" publication, I would have definitely asked for his help. Another piece of good news from the night, I managed to eat two main courses again. There is nothing like loads of free food to maintain the feelgood factor. I eventually left The Holiday Inn at 4am and actually would have stayed longer but my cough was getting really bad. I left behind a number of players and staff drinking in the bar, no doubt preparing properly for the first leg of the Play-Off Semi-Finals four days later!!

On the Wednesday evening we met at the club for the long trip to Hampshire to play Havant & Waterlooville. We were ready. The players were ready. There didn't seem to be any nerves among supporters. We arrived at the fabulous Westleigh pub attached to the Havant & Waterlooville ground and had a few drinks. By this time I was feeling awful. I'd hardly slept for the last three nights as I'd been up coughing. Paula banished me to the couch. I was starting to annoy those on the coach with my constant coughing.

My throat was starting to feel raw. Perhaps I shouldn't have come. Being dead or in a coma were the only thing that would have stopped me though!

On entering the ground I noticed what a fantastic turnout it was from Boreham Wood supporters. Two hundred and sixty of us made the trip that night, by far the biggest away following since I've been watching the club. Unfortunately for Harry, he had to miss out as it was a school night. How I wished he was there with us that night. The "Wood Army" didn't stop singing for the whole match. The players responded with a fantastic performance. They came out of the blocks and blew Havant away. Junior Morias scored a wonderful opening goal after three minutes by hitting a rasping shot from twenty yards out following a great move. Montgomery added a second after forty minutes. In between times we were the only team who looked like doing anything and should have been further in front. It was as if the Q&A ten days earlier and the Presentation Night a few days before had lifted everyone. In the second half we were less flamboyant and more solid while comfortably holding on for a 2-0 victory. We were not there yet but it would take a catastrophe for Boreham Wood not to make the final now. The second half was also lifted by the arrival of Dominos Pizzas who Havant & Waterlooville have an agreement with to supply pizza at a discounted price. Sick or not sick, a greyhound would have had trouble catching me when I heard about their arrival and I happily parted with my fiver to buy one!! We had a drink in the bar after the match and returned home in high spirits.

The following morning I couldn't wait to wake Harry up and tell him the score. He shouted "yes" quite loudly. I was feeling really rough now, almost unable to speak but managed to stumble into work only to be sent home an hour later. I had Thursday and Friday off and probably shouldn't have gone to the second leg on Saturday. When I did, I could barely speak and was unable to contribute to any singing or any drinking in the bar afterwards. We hosted Havant & Waterlooville at Meadow Park in front of a crowd of nearly a thousand people, easily our largest home crowd of the season at that stage. The performance in the first half was a bit nervy. Havant took an early lead and we went in at half time 1-0 down but leading 2-1 on aggregate. In truth the away team didn't look particularly threatening though being only one goal in front, anything could happen. On sixty three minutes the fantastic Ricky Shakes chased down a poor back pass by a Havant defender and the next thing we knew, he had an empty goal to score in. The crowd went berserk as Shakes and half the Boreham Wood team came to celebrate with them. The noise in Meadow Park reached a crescendo four minutes later when Lee Angol scored with a smart finish to give us a 2-1 lead on the day. Havant scored to make it 2-2 on the day but when the match finished, we'd won 4-2 on aggregate.

There was a mood of celebration at Meadow Park that afternoon. We still had one rather important match to go but we had the momentum. Whitehawk came through their semi-final against Basingstoke and it was the Sussex club we would face in a week's time in the final at Meadow Park. I wouldn't have wanted it any other way. I'm pleased we avoided Whitehawk in the semi-final but wanted them in the final. I was keen to avoid having to go to the "Enclosed Ground" for the play offs but was happy to see them play the final at Meadow Park against us considering they were a small club with not a lot of support. I felt that would work in our favour. The subsequent week's wait was a long one. We were only one match away from the Promised Land.

The events relating to our 2-1 victory against Whitehawk and our promotion to the National League are highlighted earlier in the book. Against all the odd, little Boreham Wood Football Club made it to the fifth tier of English football for the first time in its history.

Our fabulous new West Stand which opened in 2014

The signings of Lee Angol and Junior Morias in 2014 made all the difference

Harry is Captain against Chelmsford City in 2015

They were so sweet once!!

DREAMS OF CHILDREN

If it wasn't for Sara and Harry I would never have watched Boreham Wood FC. I would more than likely still have my season ticket at Spurs. In 2004 I decided to give up my Spurs season ticket to save money as we were trying for a family. When Sara was born in August 2005 it was obvious that it would be a number of years before I became a regular at Spurs again. There were too many financial and time restraints, like most "football mad" dads, I was always looking forward to watching my children play football and was keen to take them to watch live football. Even though my first born was a girl, I didn't see any reason why she shouldn't accompany me to White Hart Lane when the time came or play centre forward for her school team. Perhaps she would play for Spurs Ladies. If she did neither, it wouldn't be the end of the world.

On that fateful day in April 2008, I was debating what to do with two year old Sara over the weekend when I saw the promotion that Boreham Wood FC were running in the local paper offering reduced tickets for the following day's match against Carshalton Athletic. I was keen to go to the match and Paula was keen to get rid of us both for a few hours. When I told Sara that we were going to football, she was very excited. Paula dropped us at the ground the following day to watch what turned out to be an extremely boring 0-0 draw with Carshalton. Although I did watch the match, I spent most of it pushing Sara around in the pushchair. Unfortunately just before half time a non potty trained Sara did what I'd hoped she wouldn't do. The sparse crowd enabled me to change her nappy on the terrace without too many people watching. This wasn't the last time I changed a nappy on the football terrace!!

Over the next three years Sara accompanied me to a number of Boreham Wood matches mostly at home. She came with me to my first Boreham Wood away matches at Sutton United in 2009 and a few weeks later at Billericay Town. In the early days when people at the club didn't know my name, I was often referred to as "Sara's dad". Although she enjoyed coming to matches initially and saw a lot of matches home and away during the 2009-2010 promotion season, Sara soon got bored of it. As time went on, she started to have other interests and eventually stopped coming altogether. Paula had ambitious plans to have Saturday afternoons off while I took both kids to football. Unfortunately it didn't materialise that way. By the time Harry was old enough to come regularly, Sara had stopped coming. Since the 2011-2012 season Sara has only been to a handful of matches though is still quite keen to know the score when we get home from games.

The first match I took Harry to was in September 2009 against Wealdstone in the Second Qualifying Round of the FA Cup. He was eleven months old at the time and it was "fun" trying to look after him and Sara while watching an exciting game of football. A couple of months later they both accompanied me to the Ashford Town home match where Harry while munching on a bag of crisps was sick everywhere while sitting in his pushchair. I used a whole packet of wet wipes to clean him up. Fortunately that was the last we saw of Harry at Boreham Wood FC during the 2009-2010 season.

During the early part of the 2010-2011 season, Sara had a birthday party so I dragged Harry to Staines Town to watch a 0-0 draw. At this stage Harry was walking everywhere and being a clumsy sod, (as most one year olds are) he fell over and sustained a nasty graze just above his eye. Although he didn't cry much he looked like he'd just been punched. Some of the Staines supporters kept asking me if he was okay. Paula wasn't best pleased when we got home. I fully expected social services to pay me a visit!! Over the next two seasons, I took

Harry to more and more matches and although he didn't quite know what was going on, he quite liked the atmosphere. During the 2012-2013 season he started coming with me all the time including the increasing amount of away matches I was going to. The only matches he tended to miss were night games.

Although most of the 2013-2014 season was nothing to write home about, Harry was well occupied. At the time the new West Stand was taking shape and Harry watched it being built with a lot of interest. He spotted the "artists impression" of the stand in the programme and started to analyse the process in more detail then you'd expect from a five year old. When the stand had its grand opening during the pre-season match against Arsenal, Harry was proud to be one of the first people to sit in it even though, like me, he wasn't too fond of our opposition that day. Fortunately Sara and Harry have become Spurs supporters. The process of getting them to support my club was quite straightforward considering I hadn't taken either to White Hart Lane at that point.

In the 2014-2015 season Harry really came into his own as a Boreham Wood supporter. Previously he had known who some of the players were. By the early part of that season he knew who everyone was and would recognize all of them. He developed this amazing memory of previous results, what happened in matches and specific dates of matches. Harry would even remember motorway journeys when travelling to away games. During that memorable season Harry was as obsessed as the rest of us. He didn't want to miss any matches and when I had to miss a few due to weddings and stag do's Harry wasn't happy. He eventually went to the Havant & Waterlooville home match without me when I had a wedding. Harry played his part in the celebrations at the end of the season when we won promotion to the National League.

It's definitely been rewarding for me to take the kids to football. Boreham Wood FC is a close knit family club with a number of other parents taking their children to matches. The kids are certainly made to feel part of it. Perhaps it's because the Chairman has five sons of his own!!

Look what it means.

NOBODY DOES IT BETTER

Seven years is a long time with loads of different players representing the club in that period. Some have disappeared without trace, others I've forgotten about and some have been disappointing. However there are a lot of excellent players who stick in my mind. This makes my next task very difficult. It's time to pick my best X1 team who has represented Boreham Wood between 2008-2015. If I was to pick the best eleven players based on talent the whole promotion side of 2014-2015 would probably get in. Perhaps the Mario Noto of the 2010-2011 season would be hard to leave out as would Mauro Vilhete who impressed during two loan spells with us in 2012. My choice of best X1 is based on sentiment as well as talent. I'm sure you won't begrudge me five substitutes as well. Let's begin:

Goalkeeper - James Russell

An easy choice in goal. Although I'd say Tony Tucker in 2009-2010 had the best season that a Boreham Wood goalkeeper had since I've been watching them, it's hard to ignore "Rusty's" years of service. I first saw him play for Canvey Island against us in 2010 where he wished us good luck in the play offs (after we beat them). He has been instrumental in our success since joining the club in 2012. You can count the mistakes he has made on one hand.

Right Back - Ben Nunn

Another easy choice. When it was announced that Osei San-kofa was leaving the club in 2012 we had a massive hole to fill at right back. Nunn joined from Chelmsford and proved to be better than Sankofa. I'm sure that during the 2012-2015 period there wasn't a better right back in the Conference South. Nunn has everything a right back should have. He was great in the tackle and good at going up and down the line. He contributed a few important goals like the equalizer at Hayes & Yeading in that classic 2012 FA Cup match, a penalty in the 2014 Herts Senior Cup Final shootout and a late equalizer from the spot at Ebbsfleet toward the end of the 2014-15 season. We really missed him when he went travelling during the 2014-15 season.

Left Back - Mark Jones

Difficult choice as it was between him and Daniel Brathwaite. Jones joined the club from Braintree in 2011 after playing over five hundred matches for the Essex side. I didn't take to him at first but he eventually developed into a very solid dependable left back over the next three years. Although he did have some disciplinary issues in that time, talent wise he was definitely the best left back who represented the club during this period. Jones retired in 2014 and for a large part of the following season, we missed him.

Centre Back - Callum Reynolds

Simple choice. Reynolds joined in January 2012 and for the next three and a half years was our best centre back by far. He was a calming influence at the back and at no time did he look like losing his place in the side. Reynolds played well alongside a number of centre halves and I believe he made those who played alongside him, better players. He also captained the team to promotion in 2015.

Centre Back – Ryan Moran

I admit, this choice is partly based on sentiment. Moran's untimely death from cancer in the summer of 2013 at the age of thirty one was a tragedy. However he was a fantastic centre half in his time. Moran having previously been a stalwart during the FA Trophy run on 2006 returned to the club in the autumn of 2009 when key defenders like Curtis Ujah and Kevin Stephens picked up season ending injuries. Moran initially steadied the ship and towards the end of that season he produced some quite brilliant performances that meant the team only let in two goals in their final eight matches. In the 2010 Play-off Final against Kingstonian Moran produced a man of the match display. He not only kept Kingstonian's twenty eight goal forward Bobby Traynor quiet but he also scored the crucial opening goal in a 2-0 win. RIP.

Centre Midfield - Mario Noto

Easily the best player in my first three years as a supporter. He captained the team to promotion to the Conference South in 2010 and his performances in the first season at that level ensured we stayed there. Fantastic midfielder who scored plenty of goals and inspired those around him. Unfortunately injuries took their toll after 2011 but as his playing time reduced he became a successful first team coach of the promotion winning team of 2015. A club legend both on and off the pitch.

Centre Midfield - Sam Cox

Former Spurs trainee who had played with so many good players as he was breaking through. Joined the club initially on loan in 2011 from Barnet and following a one season stop over at Hayes & Yeading returned to the club permanently in 2013. Very much a fans favourite due to his work ethic on the pitch and being such a likeable guy off it. You knew what you were getting with him. He didn't score many goals but was a very good passer of the ball and rarely gave it away. Cox gave those around him an opportunity to play. He always seemed to improve as the season went on. We really missed him during his year at Hayes and Yeading.

Left Midfielder - Graeme Montgomery

As a kid I would sit in class at school not paying attention, thinking about something Glenn Hoddle did on the pitch the previous Saturday. In the last few years I've often sat at work thinking the same thing about Montgomery. He was that good. Monty is the sort of player who made you want to turn up on a Saturday. God forbid you didn't and missed something special. From when he joined the club in early 2012 he lit up the place. As his time at Boreham Wood went on, his work ethic and fitness improved while still scoring brilliant goals with that magic wand of a left foot. His goal against Farnborough on the opening day of the 2014-2015 season was the best in my years watching the club. We've been lucky to have him.

Right Midfielder - Greg Morgan

Easily the most eye catching player when I first started watching the team in 2008 and surely one of the most successful PASE graduates we have had. A very good dribbler of the ball with good pace and as the years went on his decision making improved. He spent a season at Chelmsford and returned a better player. However as the team got better and he had the likes of Ricky Shakes and Matty Whichelow competing for his spot, his first team opportunities because limited. Great servant for the club with over three hundred and fifty appearances.

Centre Forward – Lee Angol
Possibly the best centre forward to ever play for the club. When he joined the club initially on loan with his Wycombe Wanderers team mate Junior Morias, he was regarded as a raw talent. It took him a while to settle in but when he did, we saw this all action goalscoring striker that the defences at Conference South level couldn't handle. His thirty-two goals in the 2014-2015 were the key reason for the clubs promotion to the National League. I have no doubt that if Lee Angol applies himself properly, he'll have a great career ahead of him.

Centre Forward – Junior Morias
Another obvious choice due to his goals, his work ethic and his partnership with Lee Angol. When he joined us, he actually settled in quicker than Lee Angol did. Morias will always be remembered for scoring the winning goal that clinched promotion in the 2014-2015 Promotion Final against Whitehawk.

On the bench we have:

Goalkeeper – Tony Tucker
Tucker joined the club in 2009 and only had one season at Boreham Wood but what a great season that was. He was the main reason for our promotion from the Ryman League in 2010 with a string of outstanding performances. He kept twenty three clean sheets which was the joint highest amount of any goalkeeper at Ryman League level and above in the whole country. Unfortunately he left the club in the summer of 2010 and was extremely difficult to replace.

Defender / Midfielder – Luke Garrard

Garrard had been a PASE Coach for the club for a number of years before joining us permanently as a player from AFC Wimbledon in 2010. He played at right back and central midfield for a number of seasons and was a very good voice in the dressing room. He became Assistant Manager in 2012 and as the squad got better he lost his place in the team in 2015 and there was a sense that his career as a player was winding down.

Right Midfielder / Midfielder – Ricky Shakes

Joined the club in 2013 and immediately missed most of the season due to a nasty Achilles injury. When he returned to the starting line up in March 2014 it was as if the injury had never happened. Shakes proved to be probably the best player apart from Lee Angol during the 2014-2015 promotion season. He's been an all action player who has scored his fair share of important goals too.

Right Midfielder – Mauro Vilhete

Vilhete played the least amount of games out of anyone who has made this squad. However his contribution during two loans spells from Barnet in 2012 was immense. Apart from Montgomery, no player during my time watching the club had scored such outstanding goals. I was delighted for him that when he eventually returned to Barnet he scored two goals in a 2-0 victory against Gateshead at the end of the 2014-2015 season that ensured promotion back to the Football League.

Centre Forward – David Bryant

After number of years at Braintree Town, he joined Boreham Wood in February 2011 as a replacement for Ali Chaaban who joined Chelmsford. In my opinion, for the next eighteen months he because the best forward apart from Angol and Morias to have played for the club during this period. There was a period in the 2011-2012 season when he was unstoppable, scoring a succession of winners in 1-0 victories.

The line-up is:
Russell
Nunn
Moran
Reynolds
Jones
Morgan
Noto
Cox
Montgomery
Morias
Angol

Substitutes:
Tucker
Garrard
Shakes
Vilhete
Bryant

SOUNDTRACK

As you may have noticed, the book and each chapter is named after a song. If this book ever becomes a film, it would probably rival "Quadrophenia" as one my favourite film soundtracks of all time. I can only apologise for the inclusion of a Simply Red song, which has only made the list because the title is so relevant to the chapter!!

Amazing Journey – The Who
Perfect Day – Lou Reed
Start – The Jam
Why? – The Specials
Strange Town - The Jam
Empire Building – These Animal Men
Young and Innocent Days – The Kinks
Something Got Me Started – Simply Red
Knock On Wood – Eddie Floyd
You Really Got Me – The Kinks
Take Me I'm Yours – Squeeze
The Final Countdown – Europe
All or Nothing - The Small Faces
Celebration – Kool and the Gang
Who Are You – The Who
This is the Low – Blur
Calling Elvis – Dire Straits
We Can Work it Out – The Beatles
Changes – David Bowie
Wake Me Up When September Ends – Green Day

The Kids Are Alright – The Who
What's Going On – Marvin Gaye
Go West – The Village People
Getting Better – The Beatles
In The Summertime – Mungo Jerry
That's Entertainment – The Jam
Promised You a Miracle – Simple Minds
Too Much Pressure – The Selecter
Burnout – Green Day
Goodbye Cruel World – Pink Floyd
Summertime Blues – Eddie Cochran
Time for Action – Secret Affair
Orange Juice Blues (Blues for Breakfast) – Bob Dylan
After The War – Gary Moore
Rumble in Brighton – The Stray Cats
Let's See Action – The Who
Something's Gotten Hold Of My Heart – Gene Pitney
Come Together – The Beatles
Here Comes the Summer – The Undertones
It Started With a Kiss – Hot Chocolate
Get Yourself Together – Curtis Mayfield
I've Got a Feeling – The Beatles
New Year's Day – U2
We've Gotta Get Out of this Place – The Animals
Breaking Up Is Hard to Do – Neil Sedaka
You Can Get It If You Really Want – Jimmy Cliff
Broken Stones – Paul Weller
I'm Only Dreaming – The Small Faces
Dreams of Children – The Jam
Nobody Does It Better – Carly Simon
Time to Go – Supergrass

TIME TO GO

How did little Boreham Wood go from relegation to the Ryman League North to the National League in seven years?

The reprieve from relegation to the Ryman League North in 2008 due to the demise in Halifax Town FC was a stroke of luck. We had "gone down" with a wimper at the end of the season losing 5-0 away at Ramsgate when a 3-0 defeat would have saved us. If anyone deserved to go down after that performance, it was Boreham Wood Football Club. However we did have the most points of any of the relegated teams at that level so ultimately stayed up.

We had another near miss in the 2008-2009 season avoiding the trap door by two points. The promotion from the Ryman League to the Conference South in 2009-2010 was due to an excellent run of form towards the end of that season. I'm sure the Wealdstone and Sutton United teams at the time were better than us. However we only let in two goals in our final eight matches and the signing of Claude Seanla added some much needed firepower. Having gone out of the cup competitions early, the players seemed fitter than those at other clubs and the spirit in the squad was tremendous. By the time the season ended, we were "a well-oiled machine".

Having looked like going down from the Conference South in our first season at that level, a wakeup call with the thrashing by St Albans and a string of decent signings in January 2011, as well as the fantastic form of Mario Noto helped us survive quite comfortably. Between 2011 and 2014 we consolidated well in the Conference South although a dodgy spell at the end of the 2012-13 season and the beginning of the 2013-14 season led many to believe that our best days at that level were behind us. Then the loan signings initially of Anthony Jeffery and then Angol and Morias led us to safety and a Herts Senior Cup win. I think the cup win was crucial as it gave the squad a taste of success that they thrived upon and suddenly they wanted more.

Although a number of other players contributed to our promotion to the National League in 2015, there is no doubt that the signing of Lee Angol on a season long loan from Luton Town in the summer of 2014 was the icing on the cake. This signing made all Boreham Wood supporters believe this was going to be our season. The subsequent signing of Junior Morias soon after the season started was the cherry on top of the icing on the cake. Apart from David Bryant in the 2011-2012 season, we never had a goalscorer at the club during these seven years who scored anything like the amount of goals you'd expect from a decent centre forward. The defence had been very stable since 2012 with the likes of Callum Reynolds and Ben Nunn still at the club. We had players in midfield like Sam Cox and a fully fit Ricky Shakes who would run all day. We had the brilliance of Graeme Montgomery who could score a goal out of nothing. With Angol and Morias we at last had two forwards who could finish the hatful of chances we tended to create. I certainly felt, in the summer of 2014 with the signing of Angol that we had a golden opportunity to get promoted to the National League. That opportunity would be lost once he moved onto bigger and better things at the end of the 2014-2015 season. This might sound a bit negative but having taken so long to find a top quality striker; I wasn't sure how easy it would be to find another one. Had Boreham Wood failed to get promoted at the end of the 2014-2015 season I doubt we'd have gone up the following year. Without a striker of Lee Angol's quality we'd have probably finished in the top half of the table the following season but that was about it.

Off the pitch, the club is extremely well run and although the attendances are very low, there are a number of off field revenue streams that have brought money into the club. This coupled with having the same Chairman for sixteen years and the same Manager for the whole of the seven years certainly helped. There has been a clear vision in place. Vast improvements off the pitch have aided the success on it. The successful PASE scheme was expanded, the fantastic new West Stand was built and the bar and changing room areas were completely refurbished. The club certainly had a fresher feel to it in 2015 than it did in 2008.

We did have a bit of luck along the way. The reprieve from relegation in 2008 was fortunate. We avoided relegation the following season by two points. In the 2009-2010 season, more talented teams like Wealdstone imploded and didn't make the play offs. We were lucky to play Aveley away in the play-off semi-final rather than Kingstonian or Sutton. The fact that Kingstonian beat Sutton United away in the other semi-final against the odds meant we had a home final against Kingstonian rather than an away final at Sutton. In the 2014-2015 season we were very lucky with injuries and suspensions and despite a couple of tweaks here and there, we generally fielded the same side all season. We were also fortunate that Ebbsfleet United decided to change their squad half way through the season subsequently ruining their chance of challenging for the title or making the play offs. White-hawk's last minute winner at Havant & Waterlooville on the last day of the regular season meant we avoided them in a two legged semi-final and ended up playing a demoralized Havant & Waterlooville side instead. Although they were the better team, I was happier playing Whitehawk in the final at home rather than Basingstoke who were a much bigger club and would have brought treble the support that Whitehawk bought to Meadow Park. Part of me felt that Whitehawk were there for the ride and perhaps didn't have the infrastructure for promotion to the National League. Their rise had been so rapid that I thought playing in the fifth tier of English may have come too soon for them.

This book ends here I'm afraid. I hope you have enjoyed the journey as much as I have enjoyed writing my first ever book. I'm conscious that by the time you are reading this, Boreham Wood Football Club would have completed their first (and possibly only season) in the National League. I thought it was fitting to end the book at this point on a high note (and before you all fall asleep) rather than wait to add the 2015-2016 season to it. I may write a follow up about the 2015-16 season. It depends how good it is and whether there are enough things to talk about.

The period from 2008-2015 had given me a whole new perspective on football. Previously I had no interest in the "beautiful game" below league level. I remember reading the Non-League Paper in the summer of 2012 and there was an article about former Premier League forward Brett Ormerod who was than playing in the Conference for Wrexham. The headline read *Brett's not done, just reborn in the Non-League.* That headline probably sums me up!!

When I started watching the club in 2008 we were expecting to play Great Wakering Rovers and Maldon Town in the Ryman League Division One North. In the 2015/16 season we would play Tranmere Rovers and Grimsby Town in the National League. That's how far the football club I have grown to love has risen in that time. We had a few hiccups along the way but the rise up the leagues has been fantastic, nail biting and exhilarating. Despite the challenges I've faced along the way, I definitely felt this story was worth writing about. What started in April 2008, with me looking to do something on a Saturday afternoon with my daughter, has turned into an "Amazing Journey"!!

Thanks for listening.

Looking worse for wear at the end of that great day on 9th May 2015

Printed in Great Britain
by Amazon